What They *never* Taught You *in* Sunday School

a *fresh* look at following Jesus

Steven Hutson

TATE PUBLISHING, LLC

"What They Never Taught You in Sunday School: A Fresh Look at Following Jesus" by Steven Hutson

Copyright © 2006 by City Boy Enterprises
5022 Avenue N, Suite 102–128
Palmdale, CA 93551
All rights reserved.

Published in the United States of America
by Tate Publishing, LLC
127 East Trade Center Terrace
Mustang, OK 73064
(888) 361–9473

Book design copyright © 2006 by Tate Publishing, LLC. All rights reserved.

No part of this publication may be reproduced, stored in a retrieval system or transmitted in any way by any means, electronic, mechanical, photocopy, recording or otherwise without the prior permission of City Boy Enterprises except as provided by USA copyright law.

All scriptures, unless otherwise noted, are taken from the *Holy Bible, New International Version* ®, Copyright © 1973, 1978, 1984 by International Bible Society. Used by permission of Zondervan Publishing House. All rights reserved.

ISBN: 1–5988630–0-2

✠

Sometimes we are inclined to think that a very great portion of modern revivalism has been more a curse than a blessing, because it has led thousands to a kind of peace before they have known their misery; restoring the prodigal to the Father's house, and never making him say, 'Father, I have sinned.' How can he be healed who is not sick? Or he be satisfied with the bread of life who is not hungry? The old-fashioned sense of sin is despised, and consequently a religion is run up before the foundations are dug out. Everything in this age is shallow. Deep-sea fishing is almost an extinct business so far as men's souls are concerned. The consequence is that men leap into religion, and then leap out again. Unhumbled they come to the church, unhumbled they remained in it, and unhumbled they go from it.

Charles Spurgeon, 1882

table of contents

Dedication 7

Introduction 9

1: A Chance Encounter. 15

2: In Search of Clarity 23

3: The Giant Pink Elephant. 33

4: Beyond Belief 51

5: No Other Gospel. 59

6: The Great Paradox? 77

7: The Magic Potion and the Mission. 95

8: The Next Generation 107

9: My Church Has Always Done It *This* Way!. 121

10: Beware the Instant Pudding! 137

11: The Legacy of the Reformation 171

12: How Did We Get Here? 181

13: The Cost of Division 193

14: The Powerless Church 203

Epilogue: The Road Ahead 219

Bibliography 235

Endnotes 237

dedication

I planted the seed, Apollos watered it, but God made it grow. So neither he who plants nor he who waters is anything, but only God, who makes things grow. The man who plants and the man who waters have one purpose, and each will be rewarded according to his own labor.
(1 Corinthians 3:5–8)

This book is dedicated to my mother, Dorothy Gloria Lueras Hutson, for planting a small seed of faith in the heart of a young boy.

And to my grandmother, Gladys Collins Hutson, for reminding me to give thanks to the Lord before every meal.

To my many Sunday School teachers, for watering that seed for so many years.

To Daniel Donovan, for teaching me that I need the help of other spiritual men to remain close to God.

To Bill Kropp, David Owens, Bruce McPherson, Jerry Jordan, Phil Anderson, Sidney Metoyer, and Uran Chu. These men of God brought this great work to completion, in spite of my own pride and ignorance, by showing me how to get saved.

To my friend Don Patterson, a partner in the

trenches of the publishing world, for his good advice and continual encouragement.

To my wife Ruth, for her endless patience as I sit here at the computer for hours on end.

To the Lord Jesus, who makes things (including me) grow.

introduction

Blessed is the man who finds wisdom, the man who gains understanding, for she is more profitable than silver and yields better returns than gold. She is more precious than rubies; nothing you desire can compare with her. Long life is in her right hand; in her left hand are riches and honor. Her ways are pleasant ways, and all her paths are peace. She is a tree of life to those who embrace her; those who lay hold of her will be blessed.
(Proverbs 3:13–18)

This is my story. But it's not about me in particular. Change the names and a few other details, and it may also be *your* story.

I was the typical American boy growing up in the Big City in the 1960's, who had a crush on the girl next door. I went to school five days a week and competed on the swim team. On Saturday I went to the beach, the movies, or (when they were finally invented) the mall. And on Sunday, almost invariably, I went to church and to Sunday School.

Maybe you did, too.

Or maybe you're a skeptic, or a new believer. Perhaps you're still unaccustomed to this church thing, trying to make sense of it. If so, then you have an advantage over people like me—we "lifers" carry around a pile of baggage from past experiences, everywhere we go. We already have fixed assumptions on how things should be, and we stubbornly resist change. If you're just now learning about Jesus, then you're a blank slate. This can be a *good* thing if you allow it to be. This book is for you as well.

It's a survey of teaching authority and tradition, and how these things shape the way we think and worship and form opinions.

It's a sober self-examination of how well we have done in sharing that precious saving faith with the unsaved outside world.

It's a story of our common heritage in church history, an intimate unity that has given way to thousands of partisan camps.

Maybe, like me, you have likewise struggled with these issues.

The Big Question

When I was eleven years old and attending a Protestant church near my home, someone (and I don't know who) decided that it was time for me to be admitted as a member. I remember it like it was yesterday: I stood at the altar alongside the pastor during an evening service. And then came...the Big Question:

"Steven, do you accept Jesus Christ as your personal Lord and Savior?"

Pregnant pause.

So many thoughts rushed through my head. *What, exactly, did he mean by that question?* I had no idea. *What was I in for?* No one told me, and I never asked. *What was it that God expected of me?* I hadn't a clue. There was no mention of repentance, no suggestion as to what I might need to repent *of*. No talk of sin or commitment or doctrinal purity. Practically nothing, in fact, was done to prepare me for this crucial moment—except for picking out the right matching shirt and tie at Sears.

But what could I do? No time to waste; the whole world, it seemed, was watching and hanging on my every word.

I said yes.

Apparently, that was the right answer. The pastor then went on to pray for me, and presented me with my first Bible. It was a Revised Standard Version with a bright red faux-leather cover. My name was inscribed on the inside, along with the date: October 23, 1973. He welcomed me into membership in the congregation, and announced to the world that I was now a saved child of God. I was king for a day; everyone was so proud.

Hmm...it crossed my mind for barely a fleeting moment, but didn't they tell me that I was already saved through my baptism as an infant? My religious history was well-known to everyone involved, but that didn't seem to matter. No one tried to explain it. I simply followed along, because the grownups seemed to know what they were doing.

In the years that followed, I attended church almost every week. On many occasions, no one else showed up for Mrs. Johnson's Sunday School class. As a teenager I was their poster boy, representing the congregation at local and national conventions. Over time, in various places, I gave great sums of money, preached on street corners, and held various positions of leadership. I witnessed divine healings, answered altar calls, spoke in tongues, and somehow convinced people that I could prophesy. But those experiences (exciting and profound as they might be) didn't make me a Christian, and they didn't make me saved.

Maybe you can relate.

In spite of this flurry of "religious" activity, there were some very important things they never taught me in Sunday School. A Christian lifestyle means more than doing good deeds and attending a weekly church service in my best Sunday-go-to-meetin' suit. I also needed to study the Bible, learn a sound doctrine, and then teach someone else. Out with the old life and in with the new. Outward religion is not supposed to be an end unto itself, but a reflection of a person's inward condition. All of these things I never learned as a child.

I could recite the Rosary or the Lord's Prayer all day long, but I didn't know how to *pray*. I had committed to memory dozens of hymns, but rarely gave a moment's thought as to what the lyrics *meant*. I simply followed along with the crowd, and learned how to sit-stand-sit-sing-smile-chant-etc. at all the right times. And that always seemed to be enough. By all outward appearances I had always been more "religious," than most of my friends and co-workers. But I had religion, not devotion. Ritual, but not faith. Routine, but not discipline. Indeed, my early religious education was weighed on the scales and found wanting.

How about you?

This is not to say that I'm the "conspiracy theorist" type. I bring no accusation that someone lied, misled me, or maliciously withheld vital information. I have seen no evidence that large groups of clergymen join together to formulate a false or deficient Gospel for some nefarious purpose. Still, I emerged from the experience with a very incomplete understanding of what it means to be a Christian.

This is a story that had to be told. Not because my life's experiences are so unique and compelling, but rather because they are *not*. Without having to look too closely, you'll probably find your face somewhere in these pages if you went to church regularly as a child. Maybe you'll be challenged. Perhaps you'll be offended. But please bear with me.

Live the Life

The Word of God tells us that we must "watch [our] life and doctrine closely" (1 Tim. 4:16). That is, we cannot live a life that is pleasing to God until we know what His requirements are. And conversely, once informed, we must obey what we've learned. Both are equally important in the life of a Christian; neither can (legitimately) exist apart from the other. Anything else is a pious charade, just "playing church."

In another place, John warns against tampering with the Scriptures (Rev. 22:18–19). This was important for the young church, still enduring its growing pains, ever tempted to soften its tone to mollify Rome.

Sometimes our beliefs must be held immutable, not-open-for-discussion, even vital to our eternal destiny. Sometimes they're not, and we are each free to follow our own individual conscience. But how can we tell which is which? There are so many ways, it may seem, to become a Christian—a diverse universe of road maps to the Pearly Gates.

But as it happened, these issues turned out to be just the starting point for me. For as Paul experienced a life-changing vision on the road to Damascus, mine took place on the Information Superhighway. Initially, this research was intended only for my own edification. Strangely enough for a guy who has always wanted to make a living as a writer, I had no plans for a book at the time. Even so, it became a voyage of discovery that invaded nearly every area of my belief system.

Perhaps, 200 pages from now, you'll agree with some of my conclusions. Or maybe you won't. Perhaps you'll come away from the experience even more convinced of your existing beliefs. But that's okay, because I'm not necessarily trying to change your mind. I ask only that you consider a few important questions and examine some critical issues, the same ones that turned my life upside-down.

So come along, and you'll see what I mean.

✢

CHAPTER 1

a chance encounter

A river of fire was flowing, coming out from before him [the Ancient of Days]. Thousands upon thousands attended him; ten thousand times ten thousand stood before him. The court was seated, and the books were opened.
(Daniel 7:10)

It all began so very innocently, I assure you. I wasn't trying to set the world on fire, not intending to write a book. Just minding my own business on a day that was not unlike any other. And when I least expected it, *it happened...*

There was a college near my home, and they had a magnificent library. I had spent many long afternoons there, combing the stacks for books about science or art or politics or widgets, whatever happened to catch my eye that day. It was a modern building with some very traditional furnishings. On the first floor, near the Reference department, stood a vast array of elegant heavy oak reading tables. You know, the kind that you might expect to find in the Library of Congress. Here I had customarily nested for hours at a time; it was my escape from the outside world.

A few years ago, however, everything changed. One day, suddenly and without fanfare, my lair was taken away. Instead, there was a new feature—a long row of computer terminals. Dozens of them. More and more libraries were discarding their clumsy old card catalogs in favor of the newfangled electronic type. *Could it be one of those?* I wondered. Progress marches on day after day, as it must. The California State University system, which supplies so much brainpower to Silicon Valley, *cannot* be the last in the nation to go digital! Even so, I was an old dog and this was a new trick.

Upon closer examination, as it turned out, these terminals instead were connected to some kind of fancy-pants global computer network. It's called the "Internet," they told me, and you can find *anything* on it. As a taxpayer at a public institution, I was entitled to sit and surf to my heart's content—unless it got crowded, in which case everyone in the room would be required to produce a student or faculty ID. During finals week I would have been out of luck, as half the student body would be there cramming for tests. Fortunately, it was a slow day.

At long last, I had an opportunity to try out this exciting new "dot-com" technology that everyone was talking about. It was the heart of the new high-tech industry that energized the stock market and seemed poised to take over the world. But where to begin? It took a while to find my way around a Netscape browser; you know how we guys are, we'd rather drive 50 miles in the wrong direction than to stop and ask for help. But soon I was well into an exhilarating joyride in cyberspace.

Now, what to look up? Let's try religion...

Here at this mysterious keyboard something strange happened, a new revelation, if you will. There are so many belief systems out there, some of which are barely recognizable as *Christian* teachings. For starters, I found the famous bishop who wrote a book to explain why he doesn't believe in the Resurrection or the virgin birth. Apparently, by one theory, Jesus was married; by another, he was guilty of many sins. Some believe that the Bible is God's unique, authoritative Word for all time, while others accept additional books as equally trustworthy. Still others look for continuing revelation from living prophets.

(Information overload, is there no end to this data stream? Week after week, my wife pleaded with me to return home by a decent hour.)

Depending upon whom you ask, you can get saved by saying a prayer, or by merely believing in Jesus. "Just obey the Ten Commandments and you'll be saved," is one common refrain. For others, the posthumous intercessory prayers of a family member are every bit as effective. Or maybe we get saved through arbitrary preordained election, whereby God does all the work for us and it just doesn't matter what we do or think or believe.

What do all of these people with all of these opinions have in common? They all call themselves Christians. None of these issues really matter, some will tell you, as long as you believe in Jesus. And we're all one big happy family in Christ, no matter how divided we might be, whether socially, doctrinally or institutionally.

Huh?

Alas, I felt so terribly ignorant.

You see, in the course of this fascinating journey, I had read the Bible over and over again. Along the way, I had arrived at some deep convictions about what it means to become—and to live as—a Christian. Little did I know what I was getting myself into.

Into The Unknown

Very early in my experience with the World Wide Web, I happened upon a Christian chat room. Here, I was slow to pick up on the protocol and the lingo. If someone tells a joke, you can express your delight by LOL. If you have to leave the conversation for a moment, just tell your friends that you'll BRB. BTW, it's rude to TYPE IN ALL CAPS, because people will think you're shouting. And so on. This secret language was *extremely* cool, IMHO,[1] and for once in my life I was officially in with the "in" crowd.

Eventually, after a long series of false starts and blunders (remember, *real* men don't admit when they're lost), I met a friendly young woman named Katy. She was a college student in San Diego, and we chatted frequently, about once or twice a week. We laughed, we cried, we shared church horror stories. Sometimes we agreed on doctrinal issues, sometimes not. But that was okay, because we both (apparently) actually enjoyed this brave new world of virtual fellowship. In the course of this ongoing discussion we each shared our testimony. I explained that as the consummating act of my conversion, I was baptized (Greek: βαπτζω or "immersed in water") for the remission of my sins (Mark 16:16, John 3:3–5, Acts 2:38, Acts 22:16, 1 Peter 3:20–21, etc.).

Awkward moment of silence.

Au contraire, she fervently insisted. Baptism is a human *work,* she said, whereas we are saved by the grace of God. Hadn't I read Ephesians 2, for crying out loud? It is nothing more than a symbolic gesture, or an act of obedience, for a person who has already been converted and forgiven. It's a *necessary* symbol, she conceded, and one that every Christian needs to experience—but a symbol nonetheless. So I asked what she believed in. It turns out that she had attended the same Reformed church since childhood, and they were strict Calvinists. Read anything by John Calvin, she suggested, and then I would naturally understand her position. Surely the old man would set me straight.

As it happened, I knew very little about the teachings of Calvin. So at that point I snuck out of the chat room to look up the legendary 16th century French reformer in my favorite search engine. Within a few seconds (yes, I was finally mastering this strange machine), I found his historic essay *Institutes of the Christian Religion* and examined it briefly. Back to the chat room. Hmm . . ."Excuse me, do you know what Calvin said about baptism?" I quoted a small section for her. While commenting on Acts 2:38, he remarks:

> *It is his [God's] will that all who have believed be baptized for the remission of sins.*

"No, it couldn't be!" Katy exclaimed. So I e-mailed that web page to her. After reading it, she was stunned. She tried to explain it away a dozen different ways. But there it was.

Suddenly, again, the conversation became very quiet. So we agreed to disagree, and that was that. To this day (we still keep in touch periodically), despite her admiration for the Reformed teachers, my friend has not changed her opinion.

Actually, as I would learn shortly afterward, Calvin was not alone in this view of baptism. This was also the opinion of Thomas Aquinas, Jonathan Edwards, Matthew Henry, John Knox, Martin Luther, Watchman Nee, John Wesley, and practically every Christian teacher through the ages and into the Reformation era.[2] This included the Church Fathers (the earliest Christian teachers of the post-apostolic age) and the Nicene Creed, a fourth century affirmation that is subscribed by hundreds of mainstream Christian denominations to this day.

But this is not going to be a book about baptism.

Please don't get me wrong. Surely not every article of Christian teaching needs to be treated with an attitude of "non-negotiable" rigidity. We need not go about inventing new tests of orthodoxy, just to make ourselves "right" and the other guys "wrong." This kind of approach only breeds pride and hostility, and it builds walls between believers. Don't we have enough barriers already?

As the pragmatic sort, I can easily recognize

that people with strong opinions are not quickly persuaded. (Believe me, I'm just as prideful and stubborn as anyone else you know). Indeed, if you *could* be convinced to change your beliefs so easily, I'd be concerned. It would only show that you were a wishy-washy person with shallow convictions, and what good is that? It would bring no glory to God, and no benefit to you.

Naturally there will always be sincere differences of opinion within the family of God, and even the Bible allows for this (Rom. 14:1–12). So we can agree to disagree in some areas, and still remain brothers. A dogmatic attitude taken to an extreme creates a needlessly exclusive condition of fellowship. Dissent does not equal disloyalty. Choose your battles carefully.

In time, through this and other experiences, I gradually began to get the message: Many people simply don't have a good understanding of the faith that they profess. They don't know much about the doctrinal system of their church or what makes it different from the one down the street. This also became the inspiration for the book that you now have before you.

CHAPTER 2
in search of clarity

Nine out of ten adults own at least one Bible and eight out of ten consider themselves to be Christian, but you'd never know it from the smorgasbord of religious beliefs professed by most people...a large share of the people who attend Protestant or Catholic churches have adopted beliefs that conflict with the teachings of the Bible and their church.
(Barna Group survey, 2002)

On a certain occasion (Matt. 21:23–27), Jesus posed a question to the Pharisees. Did they believe that John the Baptist was sent from God? *Hmm...a trick question,* they whispered among themselves. *No matter what we say, we'll be in trouble with someone.* But no time to waste, the crowds were watching, hanging on their every word.

Their answer? A shrug.

It wasn't supposed to be this way. The Pharisees were accustomed to being on the offensive, asking the tough questions, enjoying their sport of watching the other person squirm. In the present case they could either reaffirm the Scriptures or defend their own position—but not both. So they chose a middle ground, feigning ignorance, pretending that there wasn't a problem.

With the benefit of hindsight, it's easy enough for us—who already believe in Jesus—to recognize the fallacy in their reply. *Those rotten hypocrites, playing dumb and twisting the Scriptures to justify themselves.* But wait; are not we moderns every bit as guilty?

We live in a very confusing time, where political pundits and talk-show hosts are constantly coming along with new ideas. The customary notions of life and moral values and religion have been rejected time and again. The moral absolutes of our parents' generation are ridiculed as dated and passé, and situational ethics—even among believers—have become the norm. Home-grown terrorists seeking to overthrow the U.S. government have taken to calling themselves "patriots" in the belief that they're following a higher purpose. Up is down, black is white, everything's relative, and nothing is certain.

With the passing of time, it seems our level of theological clarity has not gotten much better.

The Accidental Non-Conversion

Newly sensitized by the encounters in the chat room, I began to find great significance in other similar meetings. Often, upon meeting a fellow believer for the first time, I am eager to hear their "story," their testimony. How long have you been a Christian? How/when/where did you get saved? Truly, I have witnessed the power of God firsthand, hundreds of times, changing people's lives. How has he changed yours?

Nick, a man who came to visit my church recently, is one such example. When he joined my Bible study group for lunch at a local eatery, someone asked him the questions above. His answer? A blank stare. "What kind of question is that?" he said. "I was born into a Christian family, and I've *always* gone to church. I've *always* been a Christian!"

When encountering such a person, I sometimes feel compelled to ask: Are you married? If you are, then there must have been a point in time when you were *single*. You met a girl, fell in love, considered your options, and then *got* married...yes? Are you a doctor? If so, then there had to be a time when you *weren't* a doctor, went to school, sat for the state boards, and then *became* one—right? For every significant event in your life, you can readily identify *when* it happened, *where* it happened, and *how* it happened. There was a *process* involved, which had a beginning, a middle, and an end. You had decisions to make at various times along the way, without which the desired result would not be achieved.

But I think we can all agree that in the overall scheme of things, in the arithmetic of eternity, stuff like marital status and professional credentials will register nary a blip on St. Peter's radar screen.

So what about Nick's relationship with God, his everlasting destiny? You know, *the only thing in life that really matters?* Apparently, according to his own testimony, it just kinda *happened*. In other words, he's quite confident in his salvation, even though he can't begin to explain how—or when—or where—it occurred. Maybe his family's religion just sort of rubbed off on him, and he will be waved into Paradise along with the rest of the crowd, like a Beatles groupie with a backstage pass. Or something like that.

Some other common responses:
- "I just got saved last week, so don't expect me to be an expert."
- "My father is a minister, and he taught me everything."
- "I became a Christian 30 years ago, so I really can't recall the details."

Many people get insecure and defensive at the thought of ever having to put it into words, as if this anxiety (or possible ignorance) was a badge of honor. They might *belong* to a church, even if they rarely *attend*. They will boast of their great spirituality, as tenuous as the connections might be. And they can't really report that their life ever *changed*, because they never actually had a discernable *conversion*.

The Epidemic

The stakes could not be any greater. Still, in many churches, we find a startling level of scriptural illiteracy. Survey the pews of any local congregation, hand a Bible to a randomly chosen person, and there's a good chance that he won't be able to locate Micah or Philemon without using the table of contents. This, of course, is nothing new. It's the worst-kept secret in town, even if no one wants to admit it.

What my research has found, however, is something quite unexpected. Many believers are not particularly conversant even in *their own church*'s teachings, even if they've been a member *for their entire lives*. For the most part, even the most extensive sectarian confessions (doctrinal statements) are no more than a few pages long, and yet many have not bothered to examine even these simple documents.

Consider:

- Most of the Catholics I meet don't know the difference between the Immaculate Conception and the virgin birth.[3]
- Many Lutherans assume that Martin Luther is the founder of a church that bears his name.[4]
- I hear Jehovah's Witnesses speak of going to heaven upon their death, even though the Watchtower Society clearly teaches that every available space is already spoken for.
- Most of the Presbyterians I've met know little or nothing of John Knox, who is among the earliest and most important apologists for the Presbyterian movement.
- A few Latter-Day Saints have been incredulous when I tell them that polygamy—a practice that was once a hallowed cornerstone of their faith—is *forbidden* in the Book of Mormon. (Really! Jacob 2:24).

Once it became obvious that my research *had* to become a book, it became all the more important to get the facts straight. But that was easier said than done. Reading a book or creed by a prominent teacher was simple enough. But to understand the broader meaning of his philosophy? Well, that's another story. So just to be sure, I spent several months consulting local churches and denominational offices, either by telephone, e-mail, or "snail-mail." Some were close to home, others across the country. This approach (though admittedly unscientific) should be a reliable way to double-check some of the information from the books, websites, and other sources. If anyone can give me the scoop, it would be someone in this crowd...right? I consulted pastors, youth ministers, Sunday School teachers, secretaries, and layman volunteers who had been active members for many years.

But this wasn't so simple. Much to my surprise, for the most part, their answers were:

- "Ask someone else [our minister, our bishop, our elders, etc.]"; or
- "Read [a particular book]"; or (ironically)
- "Look it up on the Internet; our website is at www..."

Did John Hus write any books that I could consult? At the national headquarters of the Moravian Church, the secretary didn't know who to ask.

What did Mary Baker Eddy teach about salvation? The Christian Scientists couldn't tell me; they simply handed me a book, which *did not* contain the answer.

In other words, most of these people, though representing themselves as leaders in their church in one capacity or another, were either unable or unwilling to answer my questions. Apparently, the literacy rate among this group (in terms of doctrine) was not much better than the general population.

Mind you, it's not as if I go around looking for trouble or to provoke people into arguments. But as I seek to understand other points of view, these irregularities frequently arise. So if I seem especially sensitive to this issue, it's for a good reason—for the first 28 years of my life, this was *me*. I knew very little about the Bible, nothing of my own church creeds. Even so, I went about calling myself a Christian, and rejoiced very confidently in my wisdom and "salvation."

Do you *really* know what your church believes in? Do you feel secure in your standing before God?

Youthful Ambitions Rebuffed

For a short period during high school, I joined up with the debating team. My sister was already on the team, and recommended it very highly. As an eager young man with many strong opinions on any number of topics, I relished the opportunity to pontificate in front of a captive audience where no one could interrupt or leave the room. Short of a driver's license, a credit card, and a late curfew on Saturday nights, this was by far the most potent exercise of raw power and freedom that any adolescent American male could ever hope for. Look out world, here I come!

Not so fast.

Our faculty advisor, Mrs. Rattay, quickly disabused me of a few misguided notions. The purpose of debating is *not* to strong-arm people into sharing your worldview. It's not just about *talking,* but more so about *listening*. It's about the journey—fellowship with my peers, learning from one another, striving to understand their viewpoints as well. No one likes a know-it-all. So at the end of the day, it isn't about who won the argument.

"If you can't expound your opponent's position as well as he can," Mrs. Rattay explained, "then you can't really be confident in your own." The only meaningful opinion is an *informed* opinion.

I soon found this to be true. We were all edified by the experience, and developed a deep respect for one another. This approach, a painful lesson at the time, is the path that I have attempted to take in the research for this book. I sought out the advice of people who I knew did not share my views, and asked them to teach me.

Gimme That Ole Time Religion

Lest you suspect that I have come to proclaim some exotic new belief, please let me reassure you—I have no interest in doing so, because there's nothing wrong with the old one. As the old hymn proclaims, you can "gimme that ole time religion" any day. If it was good for Paul and Silas, then it's good enough for me.

But where, exactly, do we find this "ole time religion?" Maybe your church subscribes to a creed that was written 500 years ago. Is that "ole time" enough? Or maybe it was penned *a thousand* years ago. Is that better? Well, I suppose that depends on what you're looking for. Are you searching for a vindication of your existing belief system? Or do you really want to know the will of God? These questions, quite possibly, could lead to some very different answers. Sometimes, we need to step back and gain perspective to discern exactly what is Gospel, and what is simply our own cultural adaptation of it.

CHAPTER 3
the giant pink elephant

Religious truth is imprisoned in a small number of manuscript books which confine, instead of spread, the public treasure. Let us break the seal which seals up holy things and give wings to Truth in order that she may win every soul that comes into the world by her word no longer written at great expense by hands easily palsied, but multiplied like the wind by an untiring machine.
(Johannes Gutenberg, upon printing his first Bible, ca. 1455.)

Why do you believe as you believe?

Around 106 AD, the apostle John died while living in exile on the Greek island of Patmos. Upon this occasion, he took with him to the grave something very precious: a level of teaching authority that belonged uniquely to him and his fellow apostles. In time, of course, the writings of John and his peers (though not yet compiled as a Bible) would serve as the rule of faith for the church. As far as any *human* authority was concerned, however, John was the end of the line. There would never be another.

In the centuries that followed, the Church Fathers did their best to stand in the gap in the absence of a printed New Testament. Likewise, men of later generations attempted to fill this void by formulating dozens of creeds and confessions. Altogether, these teachers have influenced millions of believers through the ages. Despite their many noble efforts, however, none of them can lay claim to being an inspired prophet of God.

As believers in search of the truth, it is essential that we have a sober understanding of church history and the "evolution" of our religious teaching. Many foreign ideas have been blended with our sacred Gospel, and a host of pagan influences has been brought to bear. For this reason, it is helpful if we look beneath the surface. Then, and only then, can we have any hope of learning a sound doctrine. If we are to call ourselves Christians, then it behooves us to understand such things.

If It Ain't Broke, Don't Fix It

This matter of teaching authority cannot be over-emphasized, because it lies at the heart of everything that we do and teach and believe as Christians. It is the engine that drives our devotion; it orders our priorities and informs our moral values. It molds our character and influences our major life decisions, including how we vote and raise our children. Why do you believe in Jesus? Or how do you know that it's wrong to steal? You believe these things because someone (or some written document) told you, and at some point you accepted it as true.

But most of us learn doctrine (or at least strong opinions) in one form or another, long before we learn Scripture. We spend our formative years as human sponges, absorbing information from all sides: parents, friends, teachers, 500 channels of cable TV, popular culture, or Sunday School lessons. Perhaps you had an intensely personal, profound "religious experience" in college. Or you heard something from an evangelist at a tent meeting, and it seemed as if he was speaking directly to you and your situation.

From these experiences, we decide what we're going to believe about this subject or that. In the absence of explicit instruction, we often just follow along with what everyone else is doing, deferring to church authority or family custom without giving it a second thought. And for many of us all of this happens long before we know it, almost certainly before we ever attempt to study the Bible in any meaningful depth. The entire process is largely subconscious, almost imperceptible.

But it's there.

In my case, I approached the Bible seriously for the first time with over two decades worth of pre-existing bias already under my belt. Despite my many years of religious training, I found that many of my views were *not* vindicated by what I read. This realization hit me hard, and it left me with two options:

1) **Admit that I was wrong.** Unfortunately, though, my ego wouldn't allow this. All those years of Sunday School and I *still* didn't get it right? Please, let it be something else. Or maybe I could...

2) **Conclude that the Bible must be wrong.** In

this case, though, my *conscience* wouldn't allow it. I already knew that the Bible was God's Inspired Word, and therefore *the* authority.

These, I understood, were the only *honest* responses—but they were also highly unpleasant. So I initially settled for a third option:

3) **Interpret the Bible to my own liking**, or simply disregard the parts that I couldn't "spin" into a more pleasant message. In this manner my pride could remain intact, while I never had to face the angst that would inevitably come with openly questioning the divine origin of the Scriptures.

It is this third option that prevails among many Christians today. Nobody wants to admit it, but we all know it's true. It's the Giant Pink Elephant in the middle of the living room that no one wants to recognize. We walk around it, we feed and water it, vacuum under it, and yet pretend it's not there. For if we admitted it was there, we'd have to humble ourselves and do something about it.

Perhaps the most emphatic admonition in this matter was given by Paul, in his letter to the churches of Galatia (Gal. 1:6–9). The Galatian disciples had shown themselves to be quite impressionable when presented with exotic new ideas, and something had to be done. Paul's tone was steadfast: "If an angel should appear to you in a heavenly vision, claiming to bring a new revelation, send him away." Or even more remarkably, "Even if I myself should return to you with a different message, don't believe me either" (paraphrase mine).

Oh, that our contemporary "prophets" could possess such conviction and integrity.

The Scrabble Factor

Have you ever played Scrabble? According to the official rules, before you begin to play the game, you must choose a particular dictionary as your authority. And every player must agree with that choice. Then if your opponent tries to pull a fast one by spelling a word that you don't recognize, you can challenge him by looking it up. If it isn't in there, then he must remove the word from the board. And there is no court of appeal, because he agreed at the outset that *that* book would be the standard.

The same goes for our religious beliefs. Before we can have an honest and meaningful discussion of any particular belief, we must first agree upon what our source of teaching authority is going to be.

With this in mind, what does your church believe about salvation? Conversion? Heaven and hell? Christian lifestyle? Dating and marriage? Do you know? Think about it. Frankly, experience has shown that many people don't have a clue. Or more importantly, what do *you* believe, and why? Is it because you learned it from the Bible? Don't be too quick to answer. Before this chapter is over, you just might find it necessary to reconsider your position.

Upon further reflection, if you think about it, it just might turn out that your beliefs are actually based upon something else—parents, friends, TV, sermons, etc. We all have our own reasons for believing what we do.

So what, you ask, qualifies me to speak so boldly? It's very simple, really. For most of my life this was *me*. My personal theology was gleaned from these very sources. During the first years of my religious education, I rarely opened a Bible. Instead, my Sunday School instructors worked from the church's own proprietary curriculum. My preacher studied for years in seminary and had a diploma on the wall of his office, calling him a "Doctor of Divinity." He sounded so eloquent while quoting from his 17th-century Shakespeare-ese Bible (even though I couldn't understand half of it). He must know. Goodness gracious, we *pay* him to know, don't we? Any theological disputes among the flock were quickly settled by the simple phrase, "Well, the Pastor says . . ." and that was that. We all stood in awe of his mighty wisdom.

Surrounded by religion. So many places to turn for answers. Why should I have to read the Bible for myself? There are several clergymen of various affiliations in my own extended family, and they certainly wouldn't steer me wrong. I already have everything I need, without having to do my own homework. Oh, there had always been at least one Bible in my home, which I could consult at any time. In fact, it made such an attractive ornament on the family room bookshelf, protected by an inch-thick layer of dust.

WWJD?

No doubt, many churches (while they certainly recognize the authority of the Scriptures) nonetheless have adopted their own "authorities." When expounding their doctrine, they don't just use a Bible. Instead, they use some other "official" document. Who, or what, is *your* authority?

- Episcopalians: the *Book of Common Prayer*.
- Reformed Churches: Calvin's *Institutes of the Christian Religion*.
- Mennonites: *Mennonite Confession*.
- Greek Orthodox churches: the *Orthodox Confession*.
- Mormons: a living prophet, and the *Book of Mormon*.
- Lutherans: the *Small Catechism* and the *Augsburg Confession*.
- Methodists: the *25 Articles of Religion*.
- Celtic churches: the *Lorrha Missal*.
- Presbyterians: the *Scottish Confession*.
- Catholics: Popes, Councils, the Catechism, and centuries of tradition.
- Christian Scientists: *Science and Health, With a Key to the Scriptures*.

Hundreds of other churches—Catholic and Protestant, Pentecostal and Coptic, conservative and liberal—look to the Nicene Creed.

Interestingly, even though we cite these many disparate and incongruous sources of authority, we all call ourselves Christians. We're fond of addressing one another as "Brother" and "Sister," but how close are we really? We all claim to be following in the footsteps of the same Jesus, but are we? To answer these questions, maybe we should ask ourselves what authority *he* consulted. Do you know? The answer may surprise you:

> ***It is written:*** *"Man does not live on bread alone..."*
>
> (Matt. 4:4)

> *Isaiah was right when he prophesied about you hypocrites,* ***as it is written...***
>
> (Mark 7:6)

> ***What is written*** *in the Law?*
>
> (Luke 10:26)

> ***Is it not written*** *in your Law...?*
>
> (John 10:34)

Tempted by Satan. Indignant at the desecration of the Temple. Challenged by the unbelievers. In any and every situation, when confronted with the toughest questions, Jesus responded in one of two ways.

Parables. In some cases He would tell a parable, His own unique brand of homespun wisdom from everyday life.

Scripture. But more often than not, He found His answers in the *Scriptures*. That is, He appealed to the recognized canon of writings that even the mighty Pharisees already believed in and dared not question (at least in public). This is why He could truly say, "I have come not to abolish the Law and the prophets, but to fulfill" (Matt. 5:17).

By his own account, the Son of God possessed "all authority on heaven and on earth." (Matt.

28:18). As such, He certainly held the power to make up His own rules at any time, had He wanted to. Or He could have proclaimed new revelations from God. On the night of His arrest, He might have called down twelve legions of angels to rescue Him from an agonizing scourging and death.

But He didn't.

Instead, on just about every page of the Gospels, Jesus continually reaffirms the teachings of the prophets who came before Him. Very little of anything truly new ever came from His mouth. He allowed the Messianic prophecies to be fulfilled, though it cost Him *everything,* lest the world be forever lost.

Can you see the Giant Pink Elephant now?

The Issues

Of course, I recognize that I'm preaching to the choir; you probably wouldn't have picked up this book unless you already believed. So at this point, you just might find yourself saying something like, "Well, duh, *of course* I believe in the authority of the Bible," or "Naturally, my beliefs come from the Bible."

But did you find yourself somewhere in the listing of creeds above? If so, then the Bible's actual role in your belief system may in fact be less than you realize. Think about it.

Or to put it another way:

- Should women be allowed to preach?
- Who is responsible for bringing in new members?

- What should be done about clerics accused of ethical misconduct?
- Shall we offer weddings for homosexuals?

These issues, and others, have faced our churches in recent years. They have pitted brother against brother, caused churches to split, and caused many people to lose their faith altogether.

And how have the churches chosen to address the problem? The responses have been many and varied; they will:

- Look it up in the church constitution or Canon Law
- Search the church confession for guidance
- Launch a campaign to persuade certain key bishops to change the rules
- Convene a high-level meeting of church leaders
- Hold a hearing in an ecclesiastical court
- Look the other way, and "don't ask, don't tell."

Surely the Bible holds the answers for these questions. Clearly. In many places. Unambiguously. God knew that fallible men would lead His church, so He inspired the apostles and prophets to supply remedies for the many issues that they would face. But we mortal men seem to think we know better, so we invent new rules, new procedures, and (in some cases) a whole new bureaucracy to keep it all straight.

Jesus isn't enough? This idea of "dual authority" isn't even subtle. If someone should inquire about my religion, I tell them that I'm a "Christian." But for most people, strangely enough, this answer is not sufficient. Rather, they also expect me to tell them a brand name. This is because many believers the world over are not content to identify themselves simply as a follower of Christ. Instead, they insist upon using some denominational label. It's not enough, apparently, just to be a follower of *Jesus;* rather, it has to be Jesus *plus* some other teacher. Jesus *plus* Wesley. Jesus *plus* Zwingli. Or Jesus *plus* _____ (fill in the blank). And for many, the Bible isn't a complete source of authority. Rather, they will point to the Bible *plus* a creed or confession of some kind. Such misplaced loyalties have brought about thousands of corporate rifts over the years, and have compromised the unity of the Body of Christ.

To be fair, I don't mean to over-generalize here. Not every church (or member) regards their confession as a "source of authority." Many churches do a splendid job of teaching the Bible to their people, and the confessional documents are simply intended as doctrinal summaries for the sake of convenience.

But why would a person choose to join up with a particular church without studying (and agreeing with) its teachings? The built-in hazards of the confessions should not be underestimated.

Reformation to the Rescue?

How much do you *really* know about the Reformation? When we consider that so much of our modern Evangelical theology was framed during this period, it is important to understand where we came from.

In your Sunday School classes, at some point, they may have told you that the Reformation was a wholesale repudiation of Catholic teaching, and a return to the pure message of the Bible. Indeed, to a great extent this is true. But it's not quite that simple, because the reformers were typically very selective in their defense of the Scriptures.

Martin Luther, for one, certainly attempted to bring the Word to the common folk by producing the first Bible in the German language. This was a monumental task, and an extraordinary contribution to his countrymen, and eventually the world. He even coined an expression in Latin, which became a popular catch phrase of his era: *sola scriptura,* or "only Scripture." In other words, the Scriptures should be our only source of doctrinal authority. This sentiment and slogan are widely subscribed to among our Evangelical churches today.

Unfortunately, in practice, even a modest amount of due diligence will show us that Luther himself didn't really believe in this sacred principle. He held up the book of Romans as uniquely authoritative, calling it "the chief part of the New Testament, and the very purest Gospel,"[5] and consigned the four Gospels to a secondary status.

Among the Gospels, John was exalted as more trustworthy than the other three. Hebrews was especially problematic for Luther, and of dubious authenticity, because it seemed to contradict the others. The book of James was too works oriented, he believed, calling it "an epistle of straw." According to one account, this caused him to literally tear its pages out of his own Bible. These books, along with Jude and Revelation, were placed in an appendix because he considered them less inspired.

Sola scriptura, indeed.

Please, don't take my word for it. Next time you log on to the Internet, just go to any search engine, type in the words *"sola scriptura,"* and you'll find several thousand hits on the topic. Many of them will direct you to the official websites of churches, and many such sites will also cite their creed or confession.

We can't have it both ways; we must *choose*.

Christianity Without Bibles?

We must also be careful to remember that even during the Reformation, very few laymen could have a Bible (in *any* language) so as to examine it for themselves. Much has been said about the "conspiracy" of the Roman Catholic Church, as they forbade ordinary people from possessing one. The truth, however, is not quite so sinister. While it is true that the church suppressed the Bible, there are at least two more compelling and more significant reasons for this problem:

Technology. As far as the common man was concerned, printed Bibles simply didn't exist. Paper was scarce and ink was very expensive. The hand-copying of books was a painstaking and time-consuming process, which made it impossible to mass-produce books of any kind.

Education. The majority of people didn't know

how to read and write anyway. So there was very little demand for the books, and a precious few people qualified to copy them.

Two Steps Forward, One Step Back

It was not until the 15th century that Johannes Gutenberg appeared, displaying his new printing process with movable lead type. At last, bookmaking became relatively efficient and inexpensive. Among his first publications, of course, was the Bible. While this was indeed a revolutionary development, the book was a *Vulgate*—St. Jerome's Latin version from the 5th century.

Latin? Again, this could only reach a very limited audience, as the use of this ancient language was already very much in decline and supplanted by the regional Romance languages. And of course, this edition had a very limited run. So alas, the Holy Scriptures were still far out of reach, even for the devout and educated.

Contrary to a popular assumption, Luther's publication did *not* produce a rush of Bible reading in Germany any more than Gutenberg's did in France. Frankly, the churches could *continue* to teach just about anything they wanted, because the average man *still* didn't know any better.

Thus about 1600 years of Christianity had come and gone, and over 90% of the world's churchgoing population never held a Bible in their hands. Never had a chance to emulate the Bereans, never able to check out the message for themselves.

So when did the holy books finally become available for regular guys like you and me? Around the beginning of the 19th century, zealous Christians came forward to establish Bible Societies, which would sponsor the translation, mass production, and distribution of Bibles. Missionaries carried them everywhere. To this day, they have operations in nearly every country of the world and are still, constantly, publishing Bibles in new languages.

Josiah

For a student of the Old Testament, this story might sound familiar. In the days of the divided kingdom, the people of Judah (ostensibly the more righteous nation) had forsaken the Lord. Idol worship was rampant, and the kings and priests were increasingly corrupt. Study of the Torah was practically nonexistent.

But then King Josiah came along (2 Kings 22–23). While the temple was undergoing renovations, a priest accidentally discovered the "Book of the Law," and he brought it to the king. Upon having the book read to him, Josiah was deeply moved and tore his robes in sorrow. He was reminded of what his glorious nation *used to* stand for. He ordered all pagan symbols to be removed from the temple and had their altars destroyed. And then he renewed the covenant in the presence of all the people. Words can barely describe this momentous event.

So what was this "book," exactly? No one knows for sure. Depending on whom you ask, various scholars have speculated that it might be the book of Deuteronomy, or perhaps a complete Torah.

History Repeats Itself...Almost

So where is *our* Josiah? If ever there was an occasion to shake up the religious world, *this* (the advent of the Bible societies) was it. If there was ever a time for disciples around the world to cry out in righteous indignation and repent in sackcloth and ashes, *this* was the time.

'Twas not to be.

In the early going, the Bible Societies often faced opposition from tradition-bound churches, based upon the assumption that the typical parishioner would never be able to understand the message on his own. Nonetheless, of course, a floodgate was opened that will never be closed.

Even among the free-thinking Protestants, few people were enlightened through this development. They had never read a Bible before, so why start now? There were no widespread cheers of joy, no legions of neo-Luthers to post their grievances on church doors. Even today, in many churches, this situation has changed little; they *still* discourage (or don't actively cultivate) independent study and critical thinking.

Clearly, centuries of cherished tradition had taken their toll. Ages of conformity, sometimes enforced by the arm of the state. Reading a three-page confession is so much easier than a 1,000-page Bible. Did anyone really believe that this would change overnight, just because the people could read a book for the first time?

In a bygone era, when people had no Bibles and had to rely on a second-hand Gospel, this ignorance could be easily excused. Not so, for you and me. We are the ones who will be held accountable, both for ourselves and those we teach.

Decision Time

To be clear, I am convinced that most Christians are sincere and well-meaning, and desire with all their heart to worship God in Spirit and in truth. No doubt, most of us who call ourselves Christians would like to win the world for Jesus. Indeed, we can genuinely declare a desire to have some small part in helping to make it happen, whatever our respective roles might be.

But this calls for action.

The confessional documents identified in this chapter (along with many others) have served to divide the flock again and again. The more we place our confidence in them, the farther we drift away from God. If we really believe the Bible to be God's Word (and most of us *claim* to believe this is so), then why do we need them at all? Even if your sectarian creed can be shown to be pure Gospel, it remains a man-made document, and its authors mere men. The canon was fixed by the end of the first century, and there is no new revelation.

No man can serve two masters. As disciples of Jesus, we must de-canonize these writings and get back to the basics. As we have seen, the early church didn't need them.

Why should we?

✠

CHAPTER 4

beyond belief

*You believe that there is one God. Good! Even
the demons believe that—and shudder.*
(James 2:19)

If someone told you that they believed in the law of gravity, would you be impressed? If they said that the earth orbits the sun (and not vice-versa), would you consider them especially wise or virtuous? Probably not, because gravity and heliocentrism are simply well-established facts that are not subject to debate. The sky is blue, $E=mc^2$, and the value of π (pi) is approximately 3.14159.

Still, many people believe with all their heart that the acceptance of a historical fact (the life and ministry of Jesus) gives them an automatic free pass to salvation. They will be quick to cite the following passages:

> *"Whoever believes in him [Jesus] will not perish, but have everlasting life."*
>
> (John 3:16)

> *"Believe in the Lord Jesus, and you will be saved."*
>
> (Acts 16:31)

But that's not the whole story.

Of course, any Christian conversion must *begin* by believing in Jesus; it's the natural first step.

In John 3, Nicodemus professed a belief in Jesus. That is, he recognized Jesus as a messenger of God, even a miracle worker—but not as the promised Messiah. So his understanding was incomplete. Rather than to commend him for simply "believing," Jesus told him that he must do *more*. And before he heard Jesus utter this sentence (verse 16), Nicodemus had already heard verse 5, about the necessity of new birth. Many theories can be found concerning exactly what this "rebirth" is. Still, it is *an additional requirement* (apart from belief) that must be fulfilled.

Similarly with the story of the jailer in Philippi in Acts 16, we read that he had just witnessed a miracle of God and submitted to instruction from Paul and Silas. While we cannot know what it was they discussed, it is clear that he heard more than "just believe." Until and unless they *do* believe, there's no point in continuing the conversation! (You wouldn't baptize an unbeliever, would you?)

So if the Bible is so clear on this subject, why is there so much confusion? At least two reasons come to mind:

Cultural Conditioning. Where were you born? If it was in the United States, or most parts of Western Europe, this type of doctrine ("just believe") might seem to be a no-brainer. You live in a *Christian* nation, with a *Christian* ruler and a mostly *Christian* national legislature. The most beautiful architectural landmarks are *Christian* churches. Some of the leading colleges and universities were established as *Christian* institutions, to train ministers or otherwise spread the Gospel. Your native dialect is peppered with biblical allusions such as "turn the other cheek" (Matt. 5:39) and "go the extra mile" (Matt. 5:14). Government offices and many private businesses routinely suspend operations in honor of Christmas and Easter. In Europe and the Americas, no other religion has its holy days thus recognized. The image of Jesus is on TV, on the radio, in magazines, in movies, on the Internet—*everywhere.*

So it's almost impossible *not* to know who Jesus is. In this setting, belief in Jesus comes quite easily, the nearly reflexive product of a pervasive cradle-to-grave cultural conditioning.

But what if you came from somewhere else? What if it was someplace like Pakistan, or China, or Bahrain, or many parts of Africa, places that have largely escaped the influence of American or European culture (including religion)? If so, then there's a good chance that you were raised in a society that does not recognize Jesus as Lord, or may even be outwardly *hostile* to the faith. In fact, it may be that you'll live many years before even *hearing his name,* if at all. The simple act of believing in Jesus may be very difficult under such conditions. You will have to battle your own doubts and preconceptions, go against your culture and family traditions, and risk losing your friends. You'll endure persecution and be pressured to conform to the local customs.

Just talk to any missionary who has served in one of these places for very long. They will tell you that in such a setting, a Christian conversion is a very difficult process. Even something as simple as "belief," then, is not quite as simple as it might seem.

Give the Devil his due? I don't know about you, but in all of my 43 years I cannot recall ever meeting a person who did not believe in Jesus (that is, accepting the historical fact of his existence) even if they openly followed some other religion. So just for the moment, let's assume that you do as well. If that is the case, then you have something in common with the gang members in my old neighborhood who bear a Jesus tattoo and wear a crucifix on a gold chain. (On Sunday mornings, they would put down their guns, drugs, and spray paint cans just long enough to attend church). Likewise, Satan and his demons also believe. And let us not forget *both* sides in the ongoing civil war in Ireland. For decades, they've been hating and killing each other—by the thousands—in His name.

On the simple basis of their "belief," shall we assume that all of these people are saved Christians? Please, don't try to avoid the issue by saying something like "It's not for me to judge." You know the answer.

All things considered, the existence of Jesus is so well attested in literature and archaeology that practically no one ever tries to deny it. Even the most skeptical secular historians cannot ignore him, regardless of their own belief system. Non-Christian religions find him irresistible as well, while they strive to find ways to graft Him into their liturgy:

- Moslems believe in Jesus, but not as the Son of God. For them, he's just a wise man inferior in stature and authority to Mohammed.
- The Church of Scientology recognizes Jesus as *one part* of its "religious heritage." And this same "heritage" also includes Zoroaster (an ancient Persian prophet), Socrates (the Greek sage), and a wide assortment of other philosophies and religions.
- Unitarian Universalists believe in Jesus, but only in a loose arrangement that imposes no fixed rules and also allows each member the freedom to reject him just the same.
- Bahai's also believe, but in their system he's simply one prophet among many. Their religion is *not* mutually exclusive with any other.
- Religious Science believes in Jesus, even in his deity. But then again, they also believe that all humans are equally divine.
- Various New Age religions can be found around the world, which embrace Jesus as *one part* of their pantheist philosophy.
- Raelians, perhaps the newest world religion, believe that Jesus was literally sent from outer space; for them, He is a co-revelator alongside— and equal to—Buddha and Mohammed.
- Many ancient Roman historians and writers (Seu-

tonius, Tacitus, and Pliny the Younger) attest to the life and ministry of a Jewish prophet named "Chrestus" (very likely a corruption of the name "Christ").

Without a doubt, all of these people *believe* (that is, in his existence), with great passion and conviction. But they rob him of his uniqueness, his superiority above all others. He is relegated to a vast pantheon of prophets and philosophers, into a convenient and non-threatening package. A dash of this, a sprinkle of that, any way you want it. Just add the five magical letters J-E-S-U-S, it seems, and suddenly you're a legitimate religion. And in the end he's just another name on a piece of paper, not unlike Thor or Zeus or the Moon God.

Remember Jim Jones and the People's Temple? Heaven's Gate or the Branch Davidians? Didn't they claim to believe in Jesus? Is there anyone out there who still believes that these groups were true Christians?

The *real* Jesus, the one that is revealed in the Scriptures, is not like MSG or Polysorbate-60 or Red Dye #2. The King of Kings is not an additive that you can simply toss into a pot of stew, and season to taste. No! He is *the* way, and *the* truth, and *the* life. He is *the* Savior of the entire world, and *the* one and only way to God. And he demands, and he deserves, to be recognized as such.

All of this, of course, is terribly ironic. Through the ages, Christian teachers co-opted the customs of pagan sects, in order to attain legitimacy in the eyes of men. Today, the tables have turned; many religions have chosen to co-opt Jesus in pursuit of this same acceptance.

Let us not be so quickly impressed.

CHAPTER 5
no other gospel

I am astonished that you are so quickly deserting the one who called you by the grace of Christ and are turning to a different gospel–which is really no gospel at all...But even if we or an angel from heaven should preach a gospel other than the one we preached to you, let him be eternally condemned!
(Galatians 1:6–9)

As a child, one of my favorite television programs was "The Flip Wilson Show." Appearing weekly on the NBC network in the 1970's, Flip had a number of alter egos. One of them was Sonny, the White House janitor. Another was Geraldine Jones, the floozy. But my favorite was Reverend Leroy, the senior pastor of "The Church of What's Happening Now."

With the character of Rev. Leroy, Flip had an ingenious way of fitting a profound social commentary into a comical framework. Within this satire, he revealed some of the genuine foibles and hypocrisies in our modern church life. To be sure, our nation has many such "happening" churches, although I doubt that any of them would be glad to admit it.

In recent decades, various new trendy "gospels"

have emerged on the religious landscape of our nation. Each one begins innocently enough, by sincerely attempting to serve a particular group of people who have not been reached by "traditional" evangelistic approaches. Over time, however, they often end up emphasizing the wrong things and preaching an incomplete message.

For example:

The Feel-Good Gospel

Have you ever attended a church for the first time, and couldn't tell whether the man in the pulpit was a Christian preacher or a motivational speaker? I certainly have. His sermons are not about making you *righteous,* but instead about making you *happy.* He teaches his people not how to live a life in service to others, but instead about how to reach their goals.

Evangelist John MacArthur, while comparing this trend to a pharmacist who sold diluted (and therefore useless) medicines, remarks:

> *Sinners are asking, "What must I do to be saved?" and they're receiving the wrong answers...Instead of learning that being Christ's disciple means the world will hate them, they're learning that becoming a Christian will make them popular. Instead of hearing that following Christ requires a willingness to forsake all in this life—maybe even life itself—they are told Jesus will make them more successful.*
>
> From a letter quoted by Eternal Life Ministries, Kerrville, TX[6]

These teachers preach about heaven. They preach about salvation, blessing after blessing from God. But nary a word about the other side.

Fortunately for us, God saw this trend coming:

For the time will come when men will not put up with sound doctrine. Instead, to suit their own desires, they will gather around them a great number of teachers to say what their itching ears want to hear.

(2 Timothy 4:3–4)

Such a "gospel" would be perfectly appropriate if you were attending a seminar by Anthony Robbins, or Zig Ziglar, or Dr. Phil. That's why these men are in business, and the reason they are so successful. But the mission of a Christian church is supposed to be something entirely different.

The Prosperity Gospel

"God wants you to be rich."

"If you're *not* materially prosperous, then you're obviously unspiritual."

"You're entitled to have the best of everything, so just 'name it and claim it!'"

This is the message of the prosperity preachers.

One of the more prominent advocates of this "gospel" is Paul Yonggi Cho, the pastor of a large church in South Korea. Since the Bible tells us that all Christians are kings and priests, he reasons:

If we are kings, shouldn't we have majesty, honor, and material things befitting kings? This is our natural inheritance. It is a legacy which we can claim by showing the proper credentials. These are our treasures which we can claim as easily as we would draw money from a bank in which a generous amount of money had been deposited in our name with our account number on it.

Salvation, Health, and Prosperity[7]

Without a doubt, in our day and age, this is a very attractive message. But it is quite inconsistent with the message of the Scriptures. Jesus himself was an itinerant preacher with no possessions or fixed address (Matt. 8:20), and Peter had no silver or gold to offer a beggar (Acts 3:6). Shall we conclude that *they* were unspiritual?

In addition, the apostles consistently remind us that a Christian should live a simple life unencumbered by the burdens of worldly wealth:

> *But godliness with contentment is great gain. For we brought nothing into the world, and we can take nothing out of it. But if we have food and clothing, we will be content with that. People who want to get rich fall into temptation and a trap and into many foolish and harmful desires that plunge men into ruin and destruction. For the love of money is a root of all kinds of evil. Some people, eager for money, have wandered from the faith and pierced themselves with many griefs.*
>
> (1 Tim. 6:6–10)

So does this mean that it's a *sin* to be rich? Hardly. If you have reaped a large material reward for your hard labor, this is nothing to be ashamed of. But far from being a universal expectation of all believers, the Scriptures caution us that worldly wealth can actually cause people to *lose* their faith altogether.

The Gospel of Inclusion

Another popular philosophy which is gathering more adherents every day is the "Gospel of Inclusion." Slight variations of this teaching, also called the "Wider Mercy Doctrine," exist from place to place, but basically it means that *the whole world* is already saved and heaven-bound, period, because God is so loving and forgiving. Or in the words of Bishop Carlton Pearson, perhaps the most vocal promoter of this teaching:

> The Gospel of Inclusion is the exciting and liberating news that in the finished work of the cross, Jesus redeemed the entire world to God from the cosmic and organic sin imposed upon it by Adam, the original man. In effect, the world is already saved, they just don't know it; and, unfortunately, most Christians don't believe it. First Timothy 4:9–10 says, "...we have put our trust in the living God who is the Savior of all men, and especially those who believe." Jesus did not just die for Christians, He died to redeem, reconcile, and ultimately save the Cosmos.

According to this theory, Jesus is your Savior, regardless of whether you know who He is or actively seek Him. No matter what pagan god or golden icon you worship, the Lord will recognize and reward your devotion. Depending on who you ask, the only exceptions to this may be those who meet God, have a taste of His mercy, and then explicitly and deliberately reject Him.

Of course, Jesus has plainly refuted this notion:

> The kingdom of heaven is like a net that was let down into the lake and caught all kinds of fish. When it was full, the fishermen pulled it up on the shore. Then they sat down and collected the good fish in baskets, but threw the bad away. This is how it will be at the end of the age. The angels will come and separate the wicked from the righteous and throw them into the fiery furnace, where there will be weeping and gnashing of teeth.
>
> (Matthew 13:47–50)

The Gospel of Inclusion is a serious falsification of the *true* Gospel, and must be rejected out of hand. Our God rewards those who believe and repent and obey.

The Gospel of Easy Sexuality

Believe it or not, there was a time in our history when the issue of human sexuality was rarely discussed in church. This is because the rules were so simple: Sex is reserved for the context of a man and a woman within the bonds of marriage. Period. Sure, there were people who complained. But the churches typically held their ground.

In recent decades, this discussion has come out of the closet and into the public square. Members of the LGBT community (**L**esbian, **G**ay, **B**isexual and **T**ransgendered) are demanding a place at the communion table. At first, the issue was brought to the fore by religious groups that were already known to be "liberal" in their theology and worldview. But now, denominations of all types are coming forward to join. They may call themselves "Open and Affirming," or "Welcoming and Affirming."

One representative view:

> *Our culture needs a sexual ethic focused on personal relationships and social justice rather than particular sexual acts. All persons have the right and responsibility to lead sexual lives that express love, justice, mutuality, commitment, consent, and pleasure. Grounded in respect for the body and for the vulnerability that intimacy brings, this ethic fosters physical, emotional, and spiritual health. It accepts no double standards and applies to all persons, without regard to sex, gender, color, age, bodily condition,*

marital status, or sexual orientation...We call for...Full inclusion of women and sexual minorities in congregational life, including their ordination and the blessing of same sex unions.
("Religious Declaration on Sexual Morality, Justice, and Healing," by the Religious Institute on Sexual Morality, Justice, and Healing, Norwalk, CT)

On a similar front, on August 5, 2003, Rev. Gene Robinson was elected as the Episcopal bishop for the state of New Hampshire. This was a historic event, because for the first time an openly homosexual man was chosen to serve in such a prominent position.

But is it really possible, in the words of author Dave Shiflett, to go through life with "one foot in Jerusalem, and the other in the Castro District (the gay district in San Francisco)"?[8]

From the earliest of times, the Scriptures have exhorted us as believers to maintain our sexual purity. Examples and commands abound in both testaments, including this admonition from Paul:

I have written you in my letter not to associate with sexually immoral people—not at all meaning the people of this world who are immoral, or the greedy and swindlers, or idolaters. In that case you would have to leave this world. But now I am writing you that you must not associate with anyone who calls himself a brother but is sexually immoral or greedy, an idolater or a slanderer, a drunkard or a swindler. With such a man do not even eat.
(1 Corinthians 5:9–11)

In the Scriptures, all manner of sexual practices (outside the bond of marriage between a man and a woman) are cited and labeled as abominations before the Lord. This includes homosexuality, both among men and among women. Clearly, God cares about how you treat your body, His temple.

For many of us, it is quite tempting to vilify Rev. Robinson for his part in this situation. But this is quite unfair, because he did not *cause* the problem; he is simply the most visible figure to represent the trend. Long before his election, this "open-minded" sentiment was already brewing beneath the surface for many years. The people in the pews were deceived by their culture, and carried their worldly views into the church.

But this is not to say that all churches who preach against sexual sins are indeed following a godly path. Instead, many believers allow their own social phobias and prejudices to invade their religious beliefs. They believe that God has an especially harsh punishment in store for homosexuals, so that they might suffer doubly for their misdeeds. But as with many other beliefs, such people are reading only half of their Bible.

God hates sin, but he loves sinners. And the sin of prejudice or hate is every bit as grave as any sin of the flesh. Both of these men—the gay man and the self-righteous believer who ridicules him—need to repent and seek God's forgiveness just the same.

The "End Times All the Time" Gospel

I will never forget the first time that I heard a sermon about the end times. Eager to get a handle on this confusing matter, I went to the meeting at the invitation of a friend.

The minister cited prophecies from Daniel and Revelation, and told us with great confidence that he had identified all of the symbols. The beast is *this,* the dragon is *that,* and the world would end in *this* precise manner. The newspaper headlines would tell all. At the end of the sermon, I was utterly confused. Still, the subject captured my imagination because the preacher seemed to be so wise and insightful.

So I returned to this church a few more times. As it turned out, the pastor almost never preached about anything else. No matter how the sermon began, it always ended up with a warning about Judgment Day. We *must* have a proper understanding of the smallest details of end-times prophecy, he explained, lest we fail to recognize the signs and respond appropriately.

Nothing new. Almost from the earliest days of the church, Christians have been fascinated by the idea of seeing prophecies fulfilled in their lifetimes. They worried about the end of the world and offered up many theories. Sometimes the scenario involves a madman dictator from country X, who wields a mysterious secret weapon. Or the sun goes supernova. Or the Soviet Union would launch a nuclear strike. Whatever the theory, someone knows *exactly* how and when it's going to happen. Remember the hysteria from Y2K? Every computer in the world would crash, and Jesus would return in all His glory.

And yet somehow, dozens (hundreds?) of inevitable "doomsdays" have come and gone without incident. The Berlin Wall and the Soviet Union now exist only in newspaper clippings and history books. The Y2K bug affected almost no one. Villainous madmen have fallen by the score. (We'll have to wait and see about the sun.) The Day of Reckoning has become a multibillion-dollar industry, and attracts new customers, er, believers, every day.

And yet, somehow, we're all still here.

> Now, brothers, about times and dates we do not need to write to you, for you know very well that the day of the Lord will come like a thief in the night. While people are saying, "peace and safety," destruction will come on them suddenly, as labor pains on a pregnant woman, and they will not escape.
>
> (1 Thessalonians 5:1–3)

All of this conjecture about the end times is an exercise in futility. According to the inspired apostle, there's no point in speculating about the end, because it will come "like a thief." Jesus also used this vocabulary to describe the timing of His return (Rev. 16:15), as did Peter (2 Peter 3:10). It will come when no one expects it.

I am reminded of a bumper sticker observed on a local freeway recently:

Jesus warned us to watch for signs of the times, no question about that. But if I could tell you with absolute certainty that He would return at noon next Tuesday and take away His chosen ones with

Him, what would you do differently that you're not supposed to be doing already? Pray? Repent? Warn your neighbor? Make peace with your estranged brother/sister/friend? Evangelize? Somebody tell me, please. Because as far as I know, these are simply the ordinary duties of every Christian. We should obey the laws of God (and of the government) because it's the right thing to do, not just when we see swift justice coming around the corner.

Think about it: As a child, did you feel free to cheat on your math test when the teacher left the room? When driving down the expressway, do you stay below the speed limit only when you see a state trooper in the rear-view mirror? This kind of selective compliance at gunpoint is not a virtue; it requires no particular faith or conscience or moral compass. It is not really *obedience,* but a desperate act of running between the raindrops and hoping to stay dry. It is rooted not in a submissive respect for the law, but instead by a fear of punishment or perhaps even contempt for authority.

This obsession with end-times prophecy is almost as old as the prophecies themselves. Justin Martyr, a pagan philosopher who became one of the earliest Christian apologists, observed this controversy and wrote in response:

> *I admitted to you formerly, that I and many others are of this opinion, and [believe] that such will take place, as you assuredly are aware; but, on the other hand, I signified to you that many who belong to the pure and pious faith, and are true Christians, think otherwise.*
>
> (Dialogue with Trypho, Chapter 80)

By all accounts, the early church did not have a fixed dogma regarding the return of the Lord. Each Christian followed his own conscience, and was not stigmatized if he should hold the "wrong" view. Perhaps we should follow their example, then, and be more charitable with those who disagree.

The bumper sticker's message may elicit a chuckle at first glance, but on a deeper level it offers a stern warning. Sort of like the example of the ten foolish virgins (Matt. 25): If you wait for a particular sign before you prepare to meet the Lord, it will be far too late.

The "Great Cataract of Nonsense"

No doubt, it is very difficult to swim against the current of our culture. We learn peer pressure at a very early age in the schoolyard, and it carries over just the same into the church sanctuary. In one place, we are coaxed into cutting class and experimenting with illicit drugs; in the other, we are tempted to compromise our religious convictions. Every generation of believers has had its own struggles as they endeavor to make the faith relevant for their own era.

C.S. Lewis understood this frailty of human nature:

> *Most of all, perhaps, we need intimate knowledge of the past. Not that the past has any magic about it, but because we cannot study the future, and yet need something to set against the present, to remind us that the basic assumptions have been quite different in different periods and that much which seems certain to the uneducated is merely temporary fashion. A man who has lived in many*

places is not likely to be deceived by the local errors of his native village. The scholar has lived in many times and is therefore in some degree immune from the great cataract of nonsense that pours forth from the press and the microphone of his own age.
(*Learning in Wartime,* 1939)

What is message of the Gospel? And what is the message of the "press and microphone" for our age? *This* is the distinction that we must understand. These modern approaches, of course, are not entirely misguided. No doubt, each one serves a particular legitimate need:

- A Christian conversion, properly understood, *will* ultimately bring joy and fulfillment into the life of a believer

- Material prosperity *can,* in fact, be the fruit of a life lived in service to God

- God *does,* indeed, desire to save everyone (1 Tim. 2:3)

- We *must* repent of our past demonization of homosexuals, and reach out to them in a manner that is sensitive and respectful. Even so, they must be called upon to repent of their sin, just like anyone else

- All believers should be mindful of the end, which indeed could come at any time

No doubt, we need to have specialized ministries to reach out to different groups with different needs. Every person is at a different place in life and brings his own particular issues to the table. And we must be prepared to meet them wherever they happen to be. But as these preachers single out a particular emphasis for their ministry, they just might end up neglecting some *other* important part of the Gospel.

Winds of Non-Change

Pope Benedict XVI, shortly before his election, made it clear that he would not be quick to give in to popular demands for reform within the church. The catechism is fixed and non-negotiable, and even he himself has no authority to change it. He remarked:

> *How many winds of doctrine have we known in recent decades, how many ideological currents, how many ways of thinking...*
> *Today, having a clear faith based on the Creed of the Church is often labeled as fundamentalism. Whereas relativism, that is, letting oneself be "tossed here and there, carried about by every wind of doctrine," seems the only attitude that can cope with modern times. We are building a dictatorship of relativism that does not recognize anything as definitive and whose ultimate goal consists solely of one's own ego and desires.*
> (Pro Eligendo Romano Pontifice, 2005)

Mind you (in case you couldn't tell by now), I am not Catholic, so I don't usually follow the writings of cardinals. Even so, I believe that every Christian should take heed of this message. Benedict's firmness—hard-line and dogmatic though it might be—must be applauded.

What has become of the "Christianity" of our time? We live in an age where cheap grace is dispensed so freely and genuine devotion is so rare.

Church attendance and financial giving are down. Divorce and teen pregnancy are up. Morality is such a fuzzy concept, even among believers. These things turn us into hypocrites and diminish the true worship of our God. In my own lifetime, I don't believe I have ever encountered a professing Christian–of *any* denomination or political bent–who would disagree with this estimation.

And yet, if we attempt to defend the honor of God with any type of meaningful standard, they call us "fundamentalists." If a preacher should dare to call his people to keep the promises they make (or hold them accountable when they don't) he is quickly stigmatized as a fanatic, a legalist, or even (gasp!) a cult leader. Honest debate degrades into prejudice and name-calling.

Imagine that! How dare we actually *do* that which even the naysayers profess to *believe* in? What a blasphemous concept, to practice what we preach! Cafeteria-style religion is where it's at. After a while, *truth* is no longer the issue, because we so desperately feel the need to defend our respective institutions and win the argument. But our sacred doctrine must not be the servant of an ever-changing contemporary culture.

Conclusion

Often, when pondering the tremendous influence of these dubious "gospels," I am haunted anew by Paul's admonition to the Galatians:

To oppose my words is to oppose God.

(Gal. 1:9)

For as opinionated and dogmatic as I can sometimes be (you should have seen my first draft for this book!), I have never been so bold as to proclaim anathema upon someone who holds a different view. Yet as a prophet of God, Paul was not one to mince words. The penalty for preachers of false teachings?

May they burn in the fires of hell for all eternity.
(Gal. 1:9)

Ouch.

Mind you, I don't mean to be needlessly dramatic here. No doubt the Lord is slow to anger, and He desires that all men be saved (1 Tim. 2:14). Still, these warnings must be taken seriously.

In an era when religious belief is something increasingly individualized and experiential, it should come as no surprise that our simple faith has become so needlessly complex. Let us not be like the Pharisees, who strained out a gnat (the smallest of the unclean animals) while swallowing a camel (the largest). They made mountains out of molehills, and molehills out of mountains.

We humans are, by nature, gregarious creatures. It is quite tempting to follow the crowd. It's a lonely path when you don't fit in. Trends come and go with the wind, in religion just as surely as in hemlines. Each one quickly becomes an essential test of orthodoxy, at least for a time. But God remains unchanged.

According to the country song by Aaron Tippin, "You've got to stand for something, or you'll fall for anything." We *must* have an unmovable standard by which all other things are measured. The Greeks had a word for this; they called it a *kanon,* a type of reed that was used as a measuring stick. And this is the term that the early Christians eventually applied to the Bible. Let us recognize the beliefs and behaviors that God genuinely honors, and humbly put away the rest.

CHAPTER 6

the great paradox?

For it is by grace you have been saved, through faith—and this is not from yourselves, it is the gift of God—not by works, so that no one can boast.
(Ephesians 2:8–9)

There is a struggle that we often face as Christians. On the one hand, we are saved by the grace of God; we don't have to be perfect, because God forgives us even though we don't deserve it. On the other hand, we know that we should live righteously and serve Him with all our might. For this reason, you will find three types of Christians:

1) Those who abuse the grace of God as a license to engage in all manner of immoral behavior. *Since I'm already forgiven, it doesn't matter what I do!*

2) Out of a profound love for God, many are relentlessly works-oriented and constantly strive to be "good enough."

3) The Christian who understands the balance.

So where exactly is this balance? The answer to this apparent contradiction may have nothing to do with Scripture, or even religion. Quite possibly, the truth may lie in the limitations of your own subconscious deductive reasoning.

Let me explain. Long ago, an unknown philosopher thought up a fancy term called "false dilemma." Simply stated, this means that you see an irreconcilable tension between two points of view, when in fact they actually complement each other. For example:

Statement 1: Joe likes diet cola.

Statement 2: Joe likes pepperoni pizza.

Conclusion 1: Both of these statements cannot possibly be true, because diet cola drinkers never eat pizza, and pizza eaters never drink diet cola.

Conclusion 2: Joe, like many people, likes to drink diet cola *with* his pepperoni pizza.

Problem: Many people can never see beyond Conclusion 1.

Let us take this passage, break it down into bite-size pieces, and address each issue separately:

"It is by *grace* you have been saved ..."

When I studied writing in school, one of the most important things I learned was that a writer must define his terms. So here's a working definition for us: Grace is *unmerited favor from God*–period.

A simple one-syllable word with a straightforward definition. The apostles and the prophets, in many places, make this clear for us. Even my secular *Merriam-Webster New Collegiate Dictionary*, which has no interest in defending any particular religion, says as much. By its very nature, grace can never be earned, no matter how hard we might try. Still, this is one of the most widely misunderstood terms in the Christian lexicon. Consider:

- **Grace is not unconditional.** If it were, then *everyone* would be saved!

    > *Make every effort to live in peace with all men and to be holy; without holiness no one will see the Lord. See to it that no one misses the grace of God and that no bitter root grows up to cause trouble and defile many.*
    >
    > (Hebrews 12:14–15)

- **Grace may have an expiration date.** Even God has his limits.

    > If we [Christians] deliberately keep on sinning after we have received the knowledge of the truth, no sacrifice for sins is left, but only a fearful expectation of judgment and of raging fire that will consume the enemies of God.
    >
    > (Hebrews 10:26–27)

- **Grace is not *license*.** It is not "permission" to sin with impunity.

    > *[Since grace increases with sin] Shall we go on sinning so that grace may increase? By no means! We died to sin; how can we live in it any longer?...For we know that our old self was crucified with him so that the body of sin might be done away with, that we should no longer be slaves to sin...*
    >
    > (Romans 6:1–7)

- **Cheap grace.** Another definition of "grace" is given to us by the great Christian author Dietrich Bonhoeffer. He recognizes two kinds of grace, namely *cheap* grace and *costly* grace.

> *Cheap grace means grace sold on the open market like cheapjack's[9] wares. The sacraments, the forgiveness of sin, and the consolations of religion are thrown away at cut prices. Grace is represented as the Church's inexhaustible treasury, from which she showers blessings with generous hands, without asking questions or fixing limits. Grace without price, grace without cost! The essence of grace, we suppose, is that the account has been paid in advance; and because it has been paid, everything can be had for nothing.*
>
> (The Cost of Discipleship)

In the end, cheap grace—that which can be gained merely with words—is really no grace at all.

- **Entitlement**

As the citizens of a prosperous democracy, we Americans enjoy a large number of rights and privileges. We have the protection of the Bill of Rights, which limits the intrusion of the government into our lives. If you're poor, you can get food stamps and subsidized rent. If you belong to an ethnic minority group, you can get special consideration for a job. A criminal defendant can beat the rap if the prosecutor makes a mistake. Medical care and a college education are available for the truly needy. No doubt our society needs to have a safety net for the hungry, abused, and underprivileged.

But this system is also susceptible to a great deal of fraud. Often, people make false claims for these benefits because they feel *entitled*. They believe that someone owes them a living. And for this reason, they can never really appreciate what they have been given.

The same goes for the gift of divine grace. We

know that God is willing, even eager, to forgive our sins and shower us with untold blessings. Many people, however, seem to think they're *entitled* to be forgiven for every misdeed—no matter how heinous or habitual. So they live their lives carelessly while giving little thought to their behavior, attitudes, or doctrine. They smugly attempt to justify themselves through false piety and a selective reading of Scripture. And for this reason, they will never really appreciate the grace that they do receive.

"Through faith..."

Yes, of course, you must have faith in order to be saved; at no time in my life have I ever believed otherwise. And exactly what *is* faith? Again, a definition is in order. Fortunately, the biblical scribes have left nothing to chance. They didn't just tell us that we must have faith; they also *defined* it for us.

What it is *not*:

- Faith is not "believing." As we saw in the preceding chapter, bare belief (which naturally must *precede* faith) is quite overrated.

- Faith is not simply an intellectual agreement to a list of facts, figures, and teachings. If this were the case, then the Pharisees would be held up as paragons of spirituality.

- Faith is *not* religious conformity. If it were, then we would have to vindicate every religious sect in the world.

- It is *not* a feeling or an emotion. Otherwise, then

each of us could make up our own custom-made religion and the Lord would be obligated to honor it.

What it is:

We are told that people such as Abel, Enoch, Noah, and Abraham had great faith (Heb. 11). How do we know this? We know because the Bible says that they did more than just believe. They *demonstrated* their belief. They *acted* on their belief, and made it visible. Their deeds became the *evidence* of their faith, and that is why these men are held up as examples for you and me. So the words of James should not be surprising:

> *You see that his [Abraham's] faith and his actions were working together, and his faith was made complete by what he did...You see that a person is **justified by what he does**, and not by faith alone.*
>
> (James 2:22–24)

And then we come to the testimony of Jesus himself:

> *"I tell you the truth, anyone who has faith in me will **do** what I have been doing."*
>
> (John 14:12)

Maybe this means that we obey the explicit commands of the Scriptures. Or that we follow our Spirit-guided conscience to do the right thing in a particular situation. In any event, it is so much more than "believing."

Faith, as defined in the Bible, is *action*.

Bible tampering

For some who emphasize the "faith" connection in salvation, they will take refuge in the teachings of Martin Luther. So great was his conviction in the matter that in order to drive the point home, he would go so far as to tamper with the biblical text itself, by adding an extra word to this passage:

> For we maintain that a man is justified by faith **alone**, apart from observing the law. (Romans 3:28)

But this word *alone* is not in the original, nor is it in any Bible translation that you're likely to have read. Why the change? Luther had made a career of refuting Catholic teachings, and this unfortunate editing was probably an overreaction to the idolatry and ritualism promoted by Rome.

However, in spite of this bold stance, and unlike many of his modern-day admirers, Luther *never* used this kind of argument to diminish the importance of baptism. In fact, as we examine his writings, he has retained the *vast majority* of the Catholic dogma on salvation, including original sin and infant baptism.

Meet the Gnostics

There was a sect that began to emerge in the second century, and they were known as the Gnostics. (Almost universally, they were and are considered to be among the earliest heretics). While divided into various schools with divergent teachings, they generally held some beliefs in common. For them:

- Salvation was to be gained through special knowledge (Greek: *gnosis*) that was not revealed to other Christian groups.

- Man was created by an inferior god who was not the same as the father of Jesus.
- All material things (including the Earth) are inherently evil, and therefore must have been created by this lesser, evil deity.
- Jesus could only have been a spirit, without a physical body, and his followers simply observed a type of shared hallucination. Because flesh is evil, they forbade people to marry (1 Tim. 4:3).

The apostle John wrote of them:

> *Many deceivers, who do not acknowledge Jesus Christ as coming in the flesh, have gone out into the world. Any such person is the deceiver and the antichrist.*
>
> (2 John 1:7)

So why am I telling you about these people? Because the Gnostics—the very people who denied even the Incarnation of Christ—were the first "Christians" to teach that we are saved by *faith alone,* apart from any considerations of personal behavior. No less an authority than John himself called them "deceivers" and "the antichrist."

And yet, much of modern-day Protestantism has unknowingly co-opted their teachings.

"Not by works..."

Now let us examine the broader context of this passage, in the setting of first-century Judaism. The Pharisees, and other like-minded legalists, were in the custom of observing a host of man-made religious traditions. For example:

- They had devised, literally, *hundreds* of rules

about how to observe the Sabbath. You must do *this*. You can't do *that*. So the day of rest wasn't really restful at all.

- In a practice called *corban,* it became permissible to give money to the temple, rather than to care for one's parents in their old age—in blatant violation of the Law (Mark 7:11).
- Among the early Christian congregations, Gentile converts were compelled to be circumcised.

In short, many tradition-bound leaders had perverted the Law by teaching that godliness could be attained by simply conforming to a mountain of regulations. And many of the people believed it! True righteousness was supplanted by "religiousness." Paul (himself a recovering legalist) reminds us that no one will be justified simply by observing rules (Romans 3:20, 28).

This *mindset,* a slavery to legalism and ritual, was the bad habit that had been carried over from their former Judaism. And *this* (not any particular practice) is the problem that Paul was addressing in his letter.

Consider these Scripture verses:

> *All who are in their graves will hear his voice and come out—**those who have done good will rise to live**, and those who have done evil will rise to be condemned.*
> (John 5:28–29)

> *For we must all appear before the judgment seat of Christ, that each one may receive what is due him **for the things done while in the body**, whether good or bad.*
> (2 Corinthians 5:10)

> *My reward is with me, and I will give to everyone **according to what he has done**.*
> (Revelation 22:12)

The early Christians understood, without question, that their deeds were surely important for their salvation.

I am often perplexed when people attempt to refute the importance of baptism by quoting from Ephesians 2, because inevitably they go on to describe some other path to salvation, (such as a Sinner's Prayer). And in every case it requires some type of "work" (such as "coming forward"). Either way, you've got to make a decision to undergo the process. Either way, you need to show up. And one way or another, a certain amount of personal effort is involved. So the argument is self-defeating, because these alternative methods don't really disprove salvation by works. They simply call for a *different set* of works.

Dueling Livestock. In the Parable of the Sheep and the Goats (Matt. 25:31–46), Jesus describes the final judgment of man. Just as a farmer separates sheep from goats, likewise the Lord will one day divide the saved and the damned.

According to the classic fable, what was the difference between the two groups? Nothing is said here about their religious devotion, or that any of them were teaching false doctrines. Indeed, even false prophets may be empowered to work miracles (Matt. 7:22). Rather, the sheep (the saved) were distinguished by their *works*.

Does this mean the saved were saved *because of*

their works? No, no, a thousand times no! All other things being equal, their works became the *evidence* of a meaningful faith, the kind that moves God to remit sins.

Ritualism. In Paul's generation, as we have seen, the Pharisees considered themselves righteous because they observed *dozens* of traditions and rituals. They genuinely believed that they *could* earn favor from God in this manner, and looked down on those who didn't measure up to such an impossible standard.

And we are guilty of the same sin if we advocate *one* ritual, such as baptism? This is absurd. As we approach a sinless Messiah, no one will ever be able to *earn* their salvation.

The Almighty, in his inspired Word, tells us in several places that salvation is predicated upon faith and repentance. Depending upon your background and culture, coming to faith in Jesus can be very difficult. Likewise, repenting of your past sins can be even harder, again depending upon your particular circumstances. Walking down the aisle of a church may be a difficult chore for a person who happens to be disabled. *Baptism,* on the other hand, is *easy*. In fact, it is the only part of the conversion process that is almost entirely passive. Once you show up, someone else does all the "work."

"...So that no one can boast."

Two men went up to the temple to pray, one a Pharisee and the other a tax collector. The Pharisee stood up and prayed about himself: "God, I thank you that I am not like other men—robbers, evildoers, adulterers—or even like

> *this tax collector. I fast twice a week and give a tenth of all I get." But the tax collector stood at a distance. He would not even look up to heaven, but beat his breast and said, "God, have mercy on me, a sinner." I tell you that this man, rather than the other, went home justified before God.* (Luke 18:10–14)

Ah, the darker side of religious conversion. The new birth, fellowship with the saints, and the promise of heaven. Again, for many first-century Jews, they clearly misunderstood the meaning of salvation. This unmerited favor from above was supposed to make them ever-so-humble before the Lord of Hosts. Instead, as the Gospels illustrate, it sometimes made them boastful before other men. It's not hard to imagine that, having been *further* enlightened by discovering the Messiah, this same attitude would not be easily abandoned.

But boastfulness (while often found in religion) is not the product of any particular doctrine. It is a character trait that arises from poor training and unrepentant sin. Regardless of their church affiliation or belief system, religious folks are often among the most arrogant people that you will ever meet. It's okay, you can admit it; we all know it's true. I have been on both sides of the transaction many times. And if you've been a Christian for very long, you probably have as well.

A Christian conversion, properly understood, does not *make* a person arrogant. In fact, the very act of obeying the Gospel—to believe, come to faith, repent, and commit to living a righteous lifestyle—is probably the most profound expression of humility that any human can ever experience. Even so, a man who was a braggart *before* coming to church is likely to remain so *afterward*—unless someone teaches him differently. Perhaps even *more* so, because for a man who is predisposed to pride, his newfound faith will simply give him yet another thing to boast *about*. And as a consequence of this unfortunate example, many people reject the Gospel entirely because they don't feel welcome by the holier-than-thou contingent at church.

A Christian should be *humble?* There goes another thing they never taught me in Sunday School.

The Nature of Biblical Promises

Early in my religious education, my pastor gave me a book of Bible promises. Hundreds of promises, both Old Testament and New: Forgiveness, good health, prosperity, victory over my enemies, and so on. So many glorious things were promised to me as a Christian. But there's one small matter that he never explained: some of those promises are *conditional*. A few examples:

> ***If my people...will humble themselves*** *and pray and seek my face and turn from their wicked ways, then will I hear from heaven and will forgive their sin and will heal their land.*
>
> (2 Chronicles 7:14)

> *Then you will call upon me and come and pray to me, and I will listen to you. You will seek me and find me* ***when you seek me with all your heart.***
>
> (Jeremiah 29:11–13)

> ***If we confess our sins,*** *he is faithful and just and will forgive us our sins and purify us from all unrighteousness.*
> (1 John 1:9)

Just because a gift is conditioned on obedience, that does not make it less of a gift.

Gift or Wage? To illustrate this principle, let's suppose that a man should go to his son and tell him, "If you do your homework, I'll give you a million dollars." Suddenly motivated, the boy runs to his room to hit the books, slamming the door behind him. An hour later, Junior comes happily bounding down the stairs, math problems and book report in hand, to collect his reward. Dad inspects the papers and, true to his word, writes a check. True, there was a definite *quid pro quo* in this arrangement. But was the money a wage, or a gift?

Considering that the act was so small—and the reward so large...

Polynomials + Report on "Pollyanna" = $1,000,000

In a capitalist economy such as ours, a person's wage is (theoretically) commensurate to his productivity. The person who does more work, or does better work, gets paid more. Naturally. But how about this example? Do you know of any employer in the world with this type of pay scale? Such a huge paycheck for so little work? If so, then please let me know where I can find this company, and I promise you'll never see another book from me.

When we consider that the reward is so disproportionate to the act, it becomes clear: The money was a gift, not a wage. Therefore, the following equation should seem equally reasonable:

Belief + Faith + Obedience = Eternity with God in Heaven

Salvation is a gift that God bestows upon his followers as they believe and obey.

A Little Common Sense

In the real world, no bill collector has ever been satisfied simply because a borrower *promised* to pay. No wife has ever really felt loved by a smooth-talking husband who spent all of his time at the office. In the entire course of human history, no man has ever been exalted or remembered because of what he believed, or believed *in*. Actions, no doubt, speak louder than words.

Finally, why is it that we follow Jesus?

Is it because of something He *said?* Well, He certainly said plenty of profound things. But I don't think that's it.

Is it because of something He *believed?* Surely He believed a lot of important truths long before anyone else caught on. But no, I don't think that's it either.

Rather, it seems, we follow Jesus because of what He *did*. Lived a sinless life. Blessed and healed and raised the dead. Stood up to those who would challenge His authority. And, of course, He died for your sins and mine and rose from the grave.

Great men are great, not because of what they

say—or believe—or even shout from the rooftops. They are great because of what they *do*.

Wisdom from the East (?)

Among non-Christian religions, Hindus and Buddhists do not believe in "salvation," per se, in the sense that Christians understand it. Instead, they share in a sacred principle called "karma." (This is an ancient Sanskrit term for "action").

Many westerners, not well-versed in such matters, tend to believe that it's the same as "what goes around comes around," much as Jesus explained at Matthew 7. Or it could be expressed in scientific terms, with Newton's Third Law of Motion: "For every action, there is an equal and opposite reaction."

But that's not quite how it goes.

Under this arrangement, no one ever really dies. More precisely, it means that we all pass through an ongoing series of reincarnations, in the hope that the next life will be better than the last. Every action that you take results either in "good" or "bad" energy, which will influence your destiny. In order to assure a favorable outcome (reborn into a better situation in life), your "good" actions (karma) must outweigh the "bad." It doesn't really matter how much you "sin" in the present, because you can always fix it the next time around. It's strictly a matter of bookkeeping, manipulating the debits and credits in your account with God.

This is a far cry from the biblical concept of Heaven as final destination of eternal bliss. Karma is an endless treadmill where, even after receiving your reward, you can still lose it all at any moment. As a Christian, you probably believe that you are immune from such foolishness. But are you?

Actually, a very similar body of doctrine is quite prominent today in thousands of Christian congregations around the world. They simply have a different name for it; it's called penance. Like karma, this is a precise tit-for-tat transaction. A contrite believer, seeking to be absolved of his sins, is instructed to go out and do a good deed of some kind. Literally, this means that the virtue of this good deed will offset the guilt of that bad one. And even if you should meet your Maker before completing your penance, all is not lost—you can still be absolved in purgatory.[10]

So just how dangerous is this teaching? In the early 14th century, many wealthy people attempted to avoid penance by offering money to the church. Many priests were all too happy to cooperate, offering absolution upon payment. After a while, the church began to actively promote this option. Does this sound familiar? It should. It's called Indulgences, the very thing that led to the Reformation.

But five hundred years later, penance and purgatory remain. People try to "prove" themselves to God, and "earn" their way into heaven. They multiply ceremonies and attempt to legislate personal righteousness with many burdensome rules.

Salvation by works is alive and well.

CHAPTER 7

the magic potion and the mission

Keep on, then, with your magic spells and with your many sorceries, which you have labored at since childhood. Perhaps you will succeed, perhaps you will cause terror. All the counsel you have received has only worn you out! Let your astrologers come forward, those stargazers who make predictions month by month, let them save you from what is coming upon you.
(Isaiah 47:12–13)

Our modern debate regarding the importance of baptism can be attributed to many factors. This includes a number of common misconceptions that most people probably never think about. Much of this confusion, it seems, arises from the ancient practices of old tradition-bound churches. In their confessions, they clearly *overstate* the case. Reduced to its simplest terms, they believe that the water of the baptismal font is supposed to be some kind of magic potion with mysterious powers.

Under this arrangement, the rite can be given

only by a minister who possesses genuine apostolic succession from Peter. The church *building* must be consecrated, and the *ground* under it must be consecrated. Under most circumstances, the *water* must be duly blessed as well. The Almighty resides exclusively within the four walls, and to leave the building is to leave the presence of God. The minister's benediction must be recited according to a precise verbatim formula, as if he was a sorcerer spouting an incantation. Or the candidate must be immersed three times, once each for Father-Son-Holy Ghost. For some, you must lean *forward* into the water; for others, it's *backward*. They will baptize just about anyone, even an unbeliever, and count that person as a new convert because he got wet and went through the motions of a religious rite.

Is *this* what you believe in?

Through the years, churches grew more ritualistic and set in their ways. The *ceremony*, once understood as a means to an end, became an end unto itself. At one point in the Middle Ages, it even became commonplace to use this special water to "baptize" (consecrate) church bells. Yes, you heard me. *Bells*.

Much emphasis is placed upon the setting, with the stained-glass windows, the reverent music from the pipe organ, the imported Italian marble baptistery, and that polished copper steeple that seems to reach to the sky. Even *clothes* have become essential, and a growing industry; formal vestments for the officiant, and a baptismal gown for the candidate.

Do these things actually impart an extra measure of holiness?

In many churches, baptism is considered a sacrament (from the Latin *sacramentum,* an oath or obligation). In common usage, this is a term that means different things to different people. But for some, a sacrament is understood to be an act that *imparts* divine grace in and of itself. (This belief is also called *baptismal regeneration.*) Perhaps you've never thought about it that way, but this is exactly what many churches have been doing and teaching—yes, even *Protestant* churches—for a thousand years or more.

You say that baptism might represent salvation by works? Clearly, in this arrangement, *it is!* Saving power (allegedly) rests in water and ritual, not faith in God. But this is a far cry from the simple teaching and example of Christ and his apostles.

An Example

Some time ago, I had a neighbor who was a fellow believer. She went on vacation in Israel, and upon her return, excitedly informed me that she had just fulfilled a lifelong dream by getting baptized in the Jordan River. But wait, hadn't she already been baptized many years before? Had she not been a devoted, saved Christian since childhood? Well, yes, she explained, but *come on, we're talking about the blessed waters of the Jordan!* Indeed, this historic location is a powerful draw.

Can't afford the trip to Israel? No problem. I know of a website where they will be happy to sell you a one-ounce bottle of "holy water from the Jordan," with a certificate of authenticity. This wonderful tonic can be yours for a mere $10.00. Visa and Master Card accepted. Overnight delivery available by FedEx, for a nominal charge.

Why is this important? As Christians, we often dismiss—with self-importance and disdain—the wild ideas and superstitions of foreign religions that we don't fully understand. But in this kind of arrangement (when spiritual power is attributed to physical objects), we end up becoming just like them. And our holy faith is essentially reduced to just another pagan sect, with its own distinctive collection of rituals, icons, and talismans.

Close to Home

I can remember, not so many years ago, watching TV news stories about the many wars and conflicts around the world. Studying various foreign cultures in history class, or in National Geographic magazine. Speaking with my friends in school, who had just moved into town from distant lands. *Such strange customs in their religion,* I would think. Bowing down to idols while wearing colorful costumes. Gathering in large crowds to pray, as they rise and bow with drill-team precision. "Now isn't that silly," I would say to myself, "they're just drones, following a mindless routine."

After a while, I began to look back on my own religious history. *Isn't that what I used to do?* Whenever I went to church, I always knew what to expect, the exact same routine with the same rote prayers, sometimes reading directly from a book (*not* the Bible). Everyone knew what to do at all the right times. The announcements changed each week, but just about everything else was the same. I could probably do it in my sleep, it was so predictable.

At such a time as this, with our understanding of worship and salvation, are we really any different from pagans?

The God of Chocolate Cake

The Scriptural record is clear. Even so, baptism should not be viewed as an inconsequential matter or purely symbolic. The Bible commands baptism in many places, and a command from God is a command from God. It is binding upon anyone who claims (or desires) to be His follower. Just as we are commanded not to murder and to love one another, the command to repent and be baptized is given with precisely the same force and authority.

Jesus once described His kingdom as a banquet to which many people would be invited. No one would go away hungry or thirsty; no one would ever leave disappointed. No doubt, all of us have been entreated to share in the Lord's bounty. But this feast, as generous as it is, should *not* be confused with a cafeteria from which you can pick and choose from among many tasty morsels according to your own tastes and preferences.

I would imagine, instead, that the banquet is more like you mother's kitchen—you eat what she sets before you, or you don't eat. She gave you spinach, *because it's good for you.* She made you eat liver, because it's full of iron; and prunes, because they "keep you regular." No dessert until you finish *all* of your vegetables. Mother knew best, and eventually we all came to appreciate her wisdom.

If this concept is so easy to understand at the kitchen table, then it shouldn't be so hard to grasp at the altar of the Lord. If we desire to enjoy the chocolate cake of heaven, then we must first swallow the lima beans of humility and submission here on earth. And you might as well get used to it now, because greater challenges are sure to follow.

Or to put it another way, have you ever tried to have a case heard before the U.S. Supreme Court? There are *nine pages* of rules, just for the *format* of your petition. Count 'em, *nine!* Consider:

> *The petition and the appendix required by Rule 14 must be presented on paper that is 6 1/8 by 9 1/4 inches and not less than 60 pounds in weight...The color of the cover must be white...The petition shall be typeset in traditional Roman 11-point or larger type with 2-point or more leading between lines. Footnotes must be 9-point or larger with 2-point or more leading between lines. Please note that computer generated "Roman" type is smaller than traditional Roman type and you may need to increase the font size...*
> (Memorandum to Those Intending to Prepare a Petition, Office of the Clerk, Oct. 2005)

Some pages must be numbered with lowercase Roman (i, ii, iii, etc.) numerals, while others must be numbered with Hindu-Arabic (1, 2, 3, etc.) numerals. The cover must be 65-pound white paper. Spiral binding is not allowed; if staples are used, they must be covered with tape. And this is just the beginning. Any noncompliant petition will be returned to you before it reaches the desk of any of the justices. So the fate of your case may in fact be determined in the mailroom.

If your case was so important as to be brought before the highest court in the land, would you do it halfway (or even ¾) and think "good enough?" No, you would follow the directions to the letter! And if you're so meticulous in worldly affairs, surely you'd be no less careful in *eternal* matters.

So yes, we are saved through faith. And *faith,* as defined in the in the Scriptures, requires *action.* Without action our faith is dead (James 2:26), and therefore not really "faith" at all. Obedience to divine commands, even the details, is *everything.*

Repentance. In many places in the Bible, repentance is cited as a prerequisite for salvation. But what exactly is it? For many years in Sunday School, they told me that it means "begging forgiveness." Other people will insist that repentance is a gift from God which requires no effort on our part. They will appeal to scriptures such as Acts 5:31, or 2 Tim. 2:25, which depict God as granting repentance to people. You may even find, as I did, that some Bible reference books define this term as "a change of mind," or something similar.

A closer examination, however, will show that such views are not consistent with the whole of the scriptural record. Consider:

> *"Unless you **repent**, you too will all perish."*
> (Luke 13:5)

"**Repent**, then, and turn to God"

(Acts 3:19)

"If you do not **repent,** I will come to you and remove your lampstand"

(Rev. 2:5)

The word "repent" (Greek *metanoia*, Hebrew *shub*) literally means "to turn." In a religious context, in both cases, this indicates a turning from sin. In dozens of places in the Bible, men are commanded to repent. Why would God command us to do something if he was already doing it for us?

F. F. Bruce, an esteemed Biblical professor and author, makes the following observation:

> It would, of course, be a mistake to link the words "unto the remission of your sins" with the command "be baptized" to the exclusion of the exclusion of the prior command "repent ye." It is against the whole genius of Biblical religion to suppose that the outward rite had any value except in so far as it was accompanied by true repentance within.
>
> (Commentary on Acts)

John the Baptist warned the Pharisees to "produce fruit in keeping with repentance" (Matt. 3:8). In other words, it's not enough to just change your mind or your attitude. To truly repent, you must change your behavior. If "fruit" (results) is the test, then how can you distinguish a peach tree from a fig tree? No need for a DNA test, because the peach tree is the one that displays a clear visible manifestation—peaches. How do you know that a man has repented? No need to read his mind, because he displays a clear visible sign—a changed life.

In the words of Martin Luther:

> *Yet its meaning [repentance] is not restricted to repentance in one's heart; for such repentance is null unless it produces outward signs in various mortifications of the flesh.*
> *(Ninety-Five Theses, #3)*

Certainly, no man can repent on his own power. Yes, we unworthy mortals must beg to be forgiven. Surely the ability to repent is a gift from God. Still, it is a command that we must obey. Clearly, in our confused modern religious world, the meaning of repentance is often misunderstood. So if the "experts" tell us that repentance is merely a state of mind, it should be no surprise that the rest of us are so confused.

Perspective

Again, we must look to the apostles for precedent. In the record of Scripture, they baptized people as they deemed each one to be ready, not waiting for a special occasion or holiday. If you have believed and repented *now,* then why wait? They didn't have fancy buildings or altars. Nobody was held captive to a predetermined church "schedule," as if the work of God was controlled by a calendar or some other human manipulation. And they used whatever water happened to be available.

Mind you, there's nothing inherently wrong with stained glass, or robes, or baptizing at Easter, or whatever. If these traditions help you to feel closer to God, then by all means, carry on as usual. But please bear in mind that these are *man-made* flourishes. And if you can't imagine having a Christian church without them, then maybe it's time to reconsider exactly what it is that you've placed your faith in.

Not a Magic Potion

All things considered, it will be of no benefit to any of us if we are absolutely dogmatic about the importance of baptism. While the early church clearly affirmed that this was the *normal* channel of grace, they did not assume that He could not save any other way.

For as we have seen, many people in many places have corrupted the practice and its underlying meaning, far beyond recognition. Sadly, it now bears very little resemblance to the rite that was commanded and practiced by the Lord's apostles.

In so doing, they will portray for us an inaccurate picture of God. For them, he is a legalistic and inflexible being who cannot possibly save any other way. They will put God in a box, according to their own limited understanding; a deity who is at once omnipotent and constrained by formula.

So again, let me be perfectly clear—the physical act of baptizing people is *not* what saves them. The oceans of the world will be of no avail for a person who has not repented, or is too young or immature to understand the meaning of what he's doing. It matters not if you're standing in the Jordan, the Jabbok, or in a Jacuzzi. You can stand in a basilica, a bathtub, or on a beach. And if you haven't made a grown-up, educated decision, then *please* don't waste your time. No amount of pomp and pageantry has ever truly converted anyone, and it never will.

Properly understood, baptism is the point in time that our salvation is assured. As a wise man once told me: it's not the *what*, it's the *when*. The ritual itself (while necessary) is not the point. It's a visible manifestation of your personal faith and repentance, working in concert with the grace of God.

So is it possible to get baptized (physically) and *not* be saved? Absolutely.

CHAPTER 8
the next generation

Then little children were brought to Jesus for him to place his hands on them and pray for them. But the disciples rebuked those who brought them. Jesus said, "Let the little children come to me, and do not hinder them, for the kingdom of heaven belongs to such as these."
(Matthew 19:13–14)

Over the course of my academic career, I was never the brightest student in the class. (Okay, so I made the honor roll *once* in high school, but that was probably a mistake.) This is, I suppose, partly because I approached my schoolwork in much the same way that I approach my religion: If you explain a lesson to me—but you don't tell me how this applies to my life—I find it hard to stay interested. So if this is something purely theoretical, like the "supercollider" that those eggheads want to build in Texas, my attention will wander very quickly.

Why should it matter (for example) if I think Columbus set sail in 1493? Does that diminish his achievement in the least? Or why should I care which element is #46 on the Periodic Table? Can't I just look it up when I need it? Useless information,

I thought. Just a pretense for publishers to sell textbooks, and to give parents time to watch soap operas on TV. (And oh, by the way, #46 is palladium.)

One particular source of frustration was my 10th grade algebra class. This is something that I struggled with for a long time. Decimals, fractions, solving for *x*? Pretty straightforward, if you ask me. But working with inverse variations or negative integers? All is vanity, I tell you!

No doubt, if you give me a formula, I can always find the right answer. Following the steps in order is child's play. But figuring out the square root of the hypotenuse of -74^3? What in the world does this have to do with the price of tea in Toledo?

Let us suppose that I could, in fact, compute the answer to this problem. Then what? Would it help me figure out my cellphone bill? Would it demystify the Internal Revenue Code for us budding entrepreneurs? Someone tell me, please. Anyone?

I thought so.

My religious education was much the same. The Beatitudes (just an example) were nice enough, and my class even committed them to memory. Meekness, to be sure, was a noble virtue for a young man to cultivate. I understood that. But as a Christian with my hopes set on heaven (and with so many rewards supposedly at the Lord's disposal), why would I ever want to inherit the *earth*, of all things? That evil, polluted orb didn't seem like much of an incentive. Heaven, it appeared, was reserved for the *persecuted;* or was it? There were so many questions that I dared not ask. In my class, practically no one did.

My teachers did a fine job of passing on information, and I was pretty good at retaining it. But far too often, it was just that: *information*. Facts and figures and dates and places and such. Didn't need a church for that, I already knew how to read. So at one point I began to think, *just hand me a book, thank you very much, and I'll be on my way*. Even so, I persevered.

The message of the Beatitudes was not entirely lost on me. No doubt righteousness, mercy, and peacemaking are in terribly short supply these days. For me and my classmates, these were presented as lofty ideals; s*omeone,* certainly, must come forward and fill this void. But who? Practical application was, well, practically absent from our lessons. No one, it seemed, expected us to actually *do* this stuff.

I knew so many kids (including myself) who led double lives. We spent all week smoking or drinking or fornicating or cutting class. But we cleaned up pretty well for Sunday morning, and no one was the wiser. We knew how to work the system, to put on the "religious" hat, acting and speaking as we knew we should. And no one held us accountable; no one asked us whether we had actually lived up to the philosophy that we so loudly professed week after week. We just moved on to Matthew 6.

This problem, of course, is not unique to us baby-boomers. Parents of every generation must take heed.

The Unwitting Co-Conspirator

Raising children is a serious business, not for the faint of heart. There are so many decisions that we must make in the early years. Cloth or disposable? Bottle-fed, or straight from the source? Public or private school? Five-second rule for a dropped pacifier? Each choice carries with it a unique range of possible consequences. So often, we fear the worst. But carry on we must, and we generally find that the little ones are more durable than we knew. They come with a decent warranty from the manufacturer, even if He forgot to throw in the owner's manual.

So if you had a newborn child, would you allow him to drive your car? Would you give him wine to drink with his dinner? Let him go off to college, or get married? Should he be registered to vote in the next election?

You probably think I'm crazy for even posing these questions, don't you? Obviously, a child of that age is not prepared for such responsibilities. He needs more information, and a certain level of personal maturity. These can only come with age, experience, and education; only then will he have the capacity to make a meaningful, knowledgeable choice.

And now we come to the most important choice that any person can ever make. It's an act that makes all the others seem petty by comparison—the decision to follow Jesus for the rest of your life.

Were you baptized at a very young age? Did you have it done for your children? In many families this is a cherished occasion, a wonderful family-bonding moment that we always remember. Surely, we all want to pass down our faith to our children. But is this the way that God intended? Is it really a Christian ordinance?

Contrary to what you may have been told, the baptizing of infants and small children was unknown in the time of the apostles. The historical record shows us that the practice evolved very gradually. At first it was the rare exception, not the rule. Not until around the fourth century did the practice become widespread.

No doubt, there are many parts of the world where the average citizen has *never* heard any other opinion. In some places, your baptismal record also serves as your birth certificate; no other official documentation of births is available, even from the government. (Can you imagine a stronger endorsement of the practice?) When we examine the record of history and Scripture, however, the rationale becomes entirely untenable. It then becomes clear that these are *man-made* innovations.

Sin without sinning. Do you believe in Original Sin? Again, as with any highly consequential teaching, we must examine the lessons of our spiritual ancestors. This teaching developed slowly over time, and did not gain wide acceptance until the 5th century. A pivotal moment came when Augustine, the influential 4th-century bishop of Hippo (in northern Africa), beheld an apparent contradiction in the church's practices. On the one hand, it was universally agreed that baptism brought about the remission of sins. On the other hand, the practice of baptizing infants (who had not sinned) was gaining momentum. What to do?

The bishop proposed to resolve this apparent conflict by merging these two ideas into one. Building upon the writings of earlier Christian teachers, he postulated that all children are born with the stain of sin due to the transgression of Adam in the Garden. Hence, they would need the rite to wash away their *inherited* sin, as opposed to *actual* sin.[11] According to this position, it is impossible to believe in Original Sin without also recognizing that baptism is its remedy.

In time, as we know, Original Sin became the primary basis for the baptizing of infants and small children. Naturally, some would argue that Augustine was simply explaining a timeless truth that had always been so. History shows us, however, that the doctrine was developed in the opposite sequence.

Personal faith is needed. My seven year-old son Bradley believes in God, I'm convinced of that. On some rudimentary level he understands that God made the world, brought him into it, and took his Grandma away. And when he does bad things, it makes God unhappy. He enjoys going to church every week, sings "Father Abraham" with the other kids, recites his memory verses, and offers up a short but sincere prayer each night at bedtime. That's a good start, certainly better than myself at that age. But my wife and I harbor no illusions that he's ready to make a lifetime commitment of any kind.

Clearly, in the Scriptures, baptism must be an exercise in *your own* personal faith:

> ...having been buried with him [Jesus] in baptism and raised with him through your faith in the power of God, who raised him from the dead.
>
> (Colossians 2:12)

To answer this objection, some churches will argue that baptism actually *imparts* faith on a child. Then they will appoint baptismal sponsors (Godparents), spiritual guardians who will exercise vicarious faith for the neophyte and look after his welfare until he comes of age.

Scripture, however, knows nothing of this arrangement.

History

So if infant baptism is such an obvious mistake, how did it begin? And how has it retained its place in the liturgy? Recorded history has given us no comprehensive explanation for this development. Even so, many contributing factors can be identified. Among them:

Superstition. Early congregations kept written records of their membership (including baptisms), and some of these records have survived. In the case of infants and young children, many of them died shortly after being baptized. This has led some historians to postulate that the practice was reserved for children who were seriously ill—either in the belief that it would help them to recover, or that they might enjoy blessings in the afterlife. Or to put it another way: *they believed that water, apart from personal faith, could still save.*

Imperial command. Over time, governments increasingly got involved church affairs. Eventually, in the seventh century, the baptizing of *all* newborns was made compulsory under the Byzantine emperor Justinian. It became a crime against the state *not* to baptize every child in your family.

How Serious Is This, Really?

The impact of this trend is significant, and must be understood. One interesting case study is found in the Church of England: Year after year, over two-thirds of their baptisms are given to "infants," defined as under one year of age. Another quarter or so are "children," through age 12. That leaves just over 5% "adults" (age 13 and above) who—by the church's own reckoning—are actually able to make their own mature decision.

In other words, there was plenty of *baptizing* going on, but very little *teaching,* or *repenting,* or *converting.* No doubt there were lots of *ceremonies* happening, and many happy families. But even then the job still isn't done, because about 19 out of 20 will require a subsequent Confirmation. And if recent history is a guide, the majority will never get there. This two-step process (baptism + confirmation) is found nowhere in Scripture, or in the history of the early church. Under these circumstances, the high dropout rate should not take us by surprise.

The Twilight Zone

So what is the destiny of the baptized-but-not-confirmed? At first glance it appears that they will spend the rest of their lives in a kind of spiritual netherworld, their conversions begun but never completed. They're no longer pagans, exactly, but not yet full members. There are, I would imagine, millions of people—representing many denominations—in this situation. But hard numbers are difficult to come by, because (apparently) the churches just don't keep track of such things; or if they do, they're not talking.

I have yet to locate a church creed or confession that addresses this issue directly, and let me assure you that I've seen *plenty*. Nor have I met a clergyman who will give me a straight answer that doesn't compromise his own stated belief system. And since the Bible assumes the baptism of *contrite mature believers,* no scriptural answer exists.

But the God that I know is not a god of ambiguity. He answers "yes" or "no," not "maybe." Given the seriousness of this situation, and with so many people potentially caught up in this awkward state of suspended animation, we *must* have an answer! So when we consider the fate of these people, only two answers seem possible:

1) The child is saved anyway, because God is forgiving and gracious; or

2) The child is eternally damned, because he has failed to complete his obedience.

So what's it gonna be?

If the answer is #1, then Confirmation is actually dispensable. So why do we bother with it at all?

If the answer is #2, and *we know* from experience that the process may never be completed, then why baptize them in the first place? If the efficacy of the rite is ultimately contingent upon a future event that may never happen, then what's the point? I suppose that I would spend the first fifteen years of my child's life in a constant state of apprehension, wondering which he would choose.

So then, what happens to an unbaptized baby who dies? He goes straight to Heaven, to spend all of eternity in the presence of God. If the only barrier to salvation is unforgiven sin—and he has not sinned—then no remedy is necessary.

Plus ça change, plus c'est même chose[12]

Many unintended (even unnoticed) consequences have followed from these erroneous practices. Tradition supersedes the authority of the Scriptures. The churches claim millions of new conversions that aren't really conversions. And faith in God has been supplanted by faith in water and ritual. Far too often, after all of the ceremony, tradition, and celebration have run their course, we've failed to produce a disciple of Jesus. This no certainly no secret; you probably know someone in this situation.

Perhaps worst of all, we disrespect our children by robbing them of the dignity to make their own decisions. They may never know the joys of discovery, the struggles of repentance, or the victory of overcoming. Oddly enough, we think we're actually doing them a favor by rescuing them from these character-building experiences. So they end up learning (and passing down to *their* kids) a religion none of them really understands.

Have we learned *nothing* from the experience of our forefathers? We space-age Superchristians would like to fancy ourselves an enlightened bunch. We smugly tend to think that we have overcome the ritualism and superstition of the old ways. But have we? Sometimes I'm not so sure. Surely it is a joyous occasion whenever a child undergoes a significant rite of passage.

But let us be honest about what it means.

Follow the Leader?

So why are our children not so quick to follow us to church, as they were just a few decades ago? And once there, why don't they stick around? Maybe it's because we rely too much on the educational programs at church. Let the experts do the heavy lifting, isn't it *their* job?

Well, of course it is. But before the first theologian wrote the first catechism, *parents* were commanded to instruct their children in the ways of the Lord:

> *These commandments that I give you today are to be upon your hearts. Impress them on your children. Talk about them when you sit at home and when you walk along the road, when you lie down and when you get up.*
> (Deuteronomy 6:5–7)

No doubt, we all need a church for fellowship

and instruction. This is their mission, after all, and we all should avail ourselves of their services. And certainly, children require an extra measure of nurturing and encouragement. But in the end, that duty rightfully falls to you and me.

School prayer. Many believers (my grandmother included) are quick to blame the U.S. Supreme Court for putting an end to prayer in our public schools. Remove this daily discipline, so the argument goes, and the kids become susceptible to all kinds of errant behavior.

But that's not really what happened.

What the court decided in the 1963 case called Abington vs. Schempp is that public schools can't have an officially-sanctioned prayer session. However, if you teach your child to pray, he can pray whenever and wherever he wants. (I watch the evening news every day, and I haven't seen any reports of students being hauled off to prison for unauthorized prayer; have you?) Properly trained, Junior won't need any official prodding. Even better, voluntary *student*-led prayer groups are appearing across the land, gathering at the flagpole each morning. (Personal initiative! Isn't this what we all really want anyway?)

One Nation Under *Where?* For this reason, you will never find me picketing outside a courthouse, campaigning for the words "under God" to be retained in the Pledge of Allegiance. This is because, unless the sentiment is already in a person's heart, then repeating the words each morning will not necessarily put it there.

And while we're on the subject, what exactly is "allegiance?" What in the world is a *forwhichitstands?* At my school, it was never discussed. For me and many of my elementary school classmates, we were just chanting empty words anyway.

Granted, even the great Thomas Jefferson has affirmed that men can possess any type of political freedom, only because they have been thus "endowed by their Creator." But before this exercise can have any meaning, a person must possess a certain level of personal maturity, spirituality, and patriotism. Like the decision to follow Christ, this is heavy stuff.

Monkey Business. Likewise, I'm not especially concerned about the public schools filling young minds with that faulty science called "evolution." Do we really want our children to believe in the biblical account of Creation *just because they don't know any better?*

I can't imagine that Jesus would think so, because He expected His disciples to make an *informed* decision to follow Him. And if following Jesus means that we're a leavening influence on the lost world around us, then shouldn't we (and our children) be prepared to intelligently discuss (and refute) its false teachings? We should be able to speak their language, answer their questions, and reason with them respectfully on a level that they understand.

We should not shrink from this discussion, because it offers a wonderful opportunity for evangelism. So I say, let the schools proclaim that we came from monkeys. And for that matter, that the earth is flat, God is dead, and Elvis lives. Let the Christian kids be the smartest in the class, let them be the ones—perhaps the only ones—that know both sides of the story. Let the world know that our children are not speaking from some religious ideology or political agenda, but instead are moved by the dictates of an unshakeable conviction that's based upon real knowledge.

The world will never be won for Christ through legislation or litigation. This goal will be achieved, not by silencing the unbelievers, but by moving the Christians to speak. So let our kids speak up to their classmates. Let their lights shine before men, that every teenage knee shall bow, and every adolescent tongue confess that Jesus is Lord.

If we truly desire for our children to become committed, mature Christians, that duty falls to us. Not the teachers. Not the judges. And not your Congressman. That job belongs to you and me. Our schools have enough to do already, teaching the three R's and then waging a war against drugs and violence on campus.

Let us not make them conscripts in a battle for religious orthodoxy.

CHAPTER 9

my church has always done it *this* way!

> *It is therefore against these things that our contest lies: against the institutions of our ancestors, the authority of tradition, man-made laws, the reasonings of the worldly wise; against antiquity, custom, submission; against precedents, prodigies, and miracles. All of these things have had their part in consolidating that spurious system of your gods.*
> (Tertullian, *To the Nations*, Book 2, Chapter 1)

Tertullian lived in a world that was much different from today. As an influential leader in the church of the North African city of Carthage, he encountered many polytheistic sects that rationalized their idolatries in various ways. So what can his third-century insights offer to our modern Christian believer that worships only *one* god? Simply this—we must not allow ourselves to be carried away by tradition, worldly wisdom, and counterfeit spirituality. For these things can *become* our gods if we're not careful.

Tradition, indeed, is a very powerful force in our lives, and not just in terms of religion. In every generation of human history, men have naturally assumed that *their own* way of doing things is the best, or only, way. But in reality, every new approach is simply the most recent in a long line of passing trends. Theories and philosophies come and go with the wind, and we're slow to realize that our own ideas will someday be forgotten as well.

Giant corporations cling to outdated business models and inefficient factory designs because it's the only way they know—so they often lose out to overseas competitors. Schools continue to teach our children the same way they did 50 years ago, regardless of whether it's actually working. *That's just the way it's done!* But nothing tugs at our heartstrings and our egos quite like traditions in *religion*.

Maybe you consider yourself a faithful, strong Christian with an informed doctrine, and so you don't think this applies to you. If so, then just consider the structure of the regular Sunday worship service at your local church. How much of it is truly rooted in Scripture? If you think about it, it probably isn't much. After all, who in the first century ever heard of a choir, a pipe organ, wooden pews, amplified sound, or those little bitty cups for Communion? Could it be that the apostles wore three-piece suits, drove cars with internal-combustion engines, and deposited the operating funds in an interest bearing FDIC-insured bank account?

Frankly, upon careful examination, *very little* of what we do in the course of our corporate worship is dictated in the Scriptures. In fact, the only thing the New Testament *explicitly* calls an act of worship is offering your body as a living sacrifice. And this is a *continual* act, a matter of everyday lifestyle, not just something you do on Sunday morning.

Of course, the early church has left behind many hints for us with references to sermons, singing, group prayer, public reading of Scripture, and the Lord's Supper. And most of us have accepted these ingredients as standard and acceptable. But as for *the rest* of the meeting? *Most* of what we do in our worship services is dictated by sectarian tradition and cultural custom.

So is this *wrong?* I don't think so. Certainly, our corporate worship needs to have some type of order and structure (1 Cor. 14:26–40), as does the church "organization." Further, the Bible is silent on many of the issues and problems that we face, so we must come up with concrete, practical solutions. And no doubt, the message of the Gospel can be expressed in any number of ways to reach every nation and culture.

But as we endeavor to serve the flock, let us not be deceived into thinking we're immune from the hazards of tradition.

Papa's Predicament

I can remember seeing the movie *Fiddler on the Roof* for the first time. Tevye's three daughters wanted to get married, which was *good.* But they also wanted to choose their own husbands, which was *bad*—at least in the eyes of their father. For the eldest (who by custom *had* to marry before the others), Papa had chosen a wealthy businessman;

but she was in love with a poor tailor. What was she, nuts? Everyone knows that all marriages are arranged by the parents.

Tradition! Who were they to think they were special? Poor girls are beggars, not choosers—especially poor *Jewish* girls who had no dowry to offer.

Generations of sacred tradition had been turned on its head. What to do? Tevye was fond of quoting from "the Good Book," yet eventually realized that none of this really justified his stubbornness. So he had a grueling decision to make: Which was more important, his beloved daughters or his cherished customs? Would he allow his family to be torn apart, only to defend a practice that was *not* required either by Talmud or Torah?

In the end, Papa came around. But not without a fight, and plenty of long, hard soul-searching.

Hey, Them's Fightin' Words!

Tradition. For most of my life, that was all that I knew. Sinful at birth, an ill-defined instant conversion, and a host of other mysterious routines. If it was good enough for my parents, and their parents, and their parents, then doggone it, it should be good enough for me...right? Good Christian boys don't ask why, they just do as they're told.

Why should these traditions have such a powerful hold on us? By my count, there are at least four reasons for this trend:

Pride

As mentioned in the Introduction, I've always been religious, and from infancy have very rarely missed a week of attending a church service. I had a rudimentary knowledge of doctrine, but didn't really try to understand it. Even so, I held steadfastly to my shallow convictions. In the name of "defending the honor of God," I would valiantly go to battle with anyone who disagreed. In the process, I offended many people who now will have nothing to do with me. But as I would learn much later, the only thing that I was really defending was my own stubborn religious pride.

Lack of Initiative

If you're like me, you probably accepted the teachings of your minister or your parents at a very young age. You never questioned it, never doubted it. You just went along with it because, well, you didn't know any better, and it *seemed* right. Anything else that came along was quickly rejected because you just felt so sure of yourself. But is this really a reliable way to find the truth?

> *The first to present his case seems right, until another comes forward and questions him.* (Proverbs 18:17)

We must be humble enough to consider that the "first to present his case" *could* have been misguided. That initial lesson *might* have been incomplete or poorly understood. Of course, as we know, this kind of self-motivation is quite counterintuitive. *Complacency,* settling for the easy and familiar, is simply the natural condition of mankind.

Are you a Baptist? If so, then why are you not a Catholic? Are you an Anglican? If so, then why are you not Orthodox? Why do you attend one church and not the other? Do you know the difference? As we have seen, the distinctions are important, and they are many.

Did you make your own personal decision as an adult, after carefully examining the range of choices? Or did you just passively inherit the religion of your family, following along with generations of unquestioned custom?

Think about it.

"They're so sincere!"

"Now wait just a cotton-pickin' minute," you say. "You don't know me or my friends. The people at my church are the most sincere, committed, God-fearing, and morally upright people you'd ever hope to meet. We read our Bibles daily, pray, serve our fellow man, teach our children right from wrong, and tithe generously."

If that's the case, then by all means you should be commended for building such a model church. You were taught a certain way from infancy, and you've been devoted to it ever since. This is commendable. However, that doesn't mean that you were taught the *whole* truth of the Gospel.

Consider the example of Saul of Tarsus. He was zealous for the honor of God beyond measure. No one had better "credentials." No one had a better religious education. He knew the Scriptures as well as anyone of his generation. And in his zeal, he persecuted and killed the most dreadful heretics of all—Christians!

In time, of course, the mighty Pharisee began to see the light. Just because he was sincere and devout in his beliefs didn't mean that he was following God.

And as we know, he went on to become Paul, the most prolific missionary that the world has ever seen—but not until after he came to understand the error of his former ways.

Aristotle, the 5th century Greek philosopher and scientist, was sincere in his belief that insects sprang forth spontaneously from dirt, and the world scientific community accepted this theory for hundreds of years. Even so, to this day, he is widely regarded as one of the most brilliant scientific minds of all time.

William Miller (the father of modern-day Adventists) believed with great conviction that Jesus would return (and the world would end) in 1844. While this date came and went without incident, he attracted a following that today numbers in the millions.

Sincerity is not the issue. Devotion is not the issue. Good intentions in the face of copious evidence to the contrary avail nothing. If nothing else, the lessons of history should remind us that "religiousness" is not enough.

Church Mandate

In the aftermath of the Reformation, the Roman Catholic Church found itself in a defensive position on many fronts. In particular, a growing chorus of dissidents complained that the church promoted teachings that were contrary to Scripture. At a council held in the Northern Italian city of Trent, the assembled bishops steadfastly reaffirmed their stance with this statement:

> Following the examples of the orthodox Fathers, [the

> *Council] receives and venerates with an equal affection of piety and reverence, all the books both of the Old and of the New Testament—seeing that one God is the author of both—as also the said [unwritten] traditions, as well those appertaining to faith as to morals, as having been dictated, either by Christ's own word of mouth, or by the Holy Ghost...*
>
> (Fourth Session)

Put simply, the church began to teach that its own traditions were equally authoritative with the Scriptures. But this type of arrangement is fraught with many dangers:

Jesus explicitly refuted this doctrine. On one occasion, the Pharisees rebuked Jesus and His disciples for eating with unwashed (therefore ceremonially "unclean") hands, in violation of a time-honored tradition. He stood accused of violating not Holy Writ, but the contrived rules of the religious establishment. This breach of protocol, they believed, was itself tantamount to sin.

In predictable fashion, Jesus countered them by quoting from a prophet:

> *Thus you nullify the word of God for the sake of your tradition. You hypocrites! Isaiah was right when he said about you . . ." They worship me in vain; their teachings are but rules taught by men."*
>
> (Matthew 15:6–9)

He admonishes them (and us) that our worship of God must be in accordance with the Scriptures and not our religious traditions.

It's dishonest. This idea of dual authority is inherently deceitful. Many times, when I have inquired of my friends of other faiths, the conversation goes something like this:

"What would you do if you read something in the Bible that contradicted what they told you at church?"

"My church wouldn't do that."

"Well, what if they *did?*"

"But they wouldn't."

And so on.

The trouble is, once you've accepted this type of premise, you will eventually find a contradiction between the two authorities. So in order to resolve the conflict, you will need to choose one over the other. Sooner or later, one of the two will have to prevail.

And lastly, what is a tradition? It is an entrenched religious custom. So for the sake of discussion, let's suppose that you went to church tomorrow and the local bishop announced that he was introducing a new rule requiring everyone to wear a purple hat whenever they come to church.

Some of the people find it silly, even absurd; but because it isn't quite so burdensome and they respect their church leaders, they follow along quietly.

Thirty years from now, the church will have raised up a whole new generation of believers who never knew the old ways. For them, the purple hat policy is just a natural part of the landscape.

So by now this man-made rule has become *tradition*. As far as the people are concerned, it is a solemn command of God. And the church can use this policy (tradition = Scripture) to create and enforce any kind of doctrine or practice they like.

Sounds dangerous to me.

So shall we conclude that all traditions are *bad?* No, of course not. But if we should ascribe primacy to our own sectarian customs, our attempt at worship is futile (see Matt. 15, above). It is useless. You might as well stay in bed on Sunday morning or watch the big game on TV, because it won't do you any good to go to church.

Legalism

Legalism kills.

Bob Russell is the pastor of a vibrant, growing church in Louisville, Kentucky. In his book *When God Builds a Church,* he points out that tradition often leads to a spirit of legalism. A liberal wants to change *everything,* whereas the legalist is willing to change *nothing.* The legalist truly believes that he is defending the truth, when in fact he is only defending his traditions. The liberal, while attempting to counteract the chaff of the legalist, may in fact be discarding some valuable grain as well. Both of these people are equally dangerous in the life of a church.

In his book, Russell cites a survey that studied the effects of legalism. Among churches that were losing members and dying, fully one-half of the people described their church as "tradition-bound." We tell our people that they have been freed from sin because of the sacrifice of Jesus on the cross.

And then we turn around and make them slaves to a pile of traditions!

It was *legalism,* a desperate attempt to cling to the past in the face of changing times, which caused some early churches to have their Gentile converts circumcised. It was *legalism* and an unwillingness to recognize the deeper meaning of the Law that led the Pharisees to rebuke Jesus for healing on the Sabbath. Today, a legalistic spirit inhabits many of our churches, as they defend the past while failing to meet the needs of the souls in their care *now.*

Time-honored hymns, or contemporary choruses? Grand cathedrals or home cell groups? Old-fashioned Bible version, or modern translation? In the eyes of the Almighty, I can't imagine that it matters. Our mission is to save the world; just about everything else is details. Even so, people frequently insist upon having it one way or the other, and divide themselves accordingly.

State-Sponsored Legalism. Many years ago, when visiting my father's family in Austin, Texas, I didn't want to return home without some type of souvenir for my friends. After much consideration I chose to get a case of Pearl beer, a locally produced brand. So my cousin directed me to a local market, where I picked up the package and headed for the checkout counter. But the cashier wouldn't sell it to me.

I scratch my head. *Maybe this county prefers Confederate currency over my Yankee greenbacks?*

The cashier, it seemed, quickly pegged me as

an out-of-towner. He explained that Texas is one of several states that still observe the "Blue Law." This is a body of legislation that was enacted in various forms throughout the South decades ago. By one account, it was patterned after the laws of 18th century Puritan England (supposedly printed on blue paper, for some reason), which attempted to impose religiously-oriented values on the citizenry by force. Among other things, this policy places tight restrictions on the distribution and sale of alcoholic beverages.

Some parts of the Blue Law are no longer enforced, or have been repealed altogether. But one of the surviving provisions of the law (Alcoholic Beverage Code, Chapter 105) is that you can't buy beer in Texas on Sunday before noon. Sunday morning is supposed to be church time. And I was almost an hour early.

Of course, this is nothing new. This form of counterfeit righteousness was observed in the days of the apostles:

> *Since you died with Christ to the basic principles of this world, why, as though you still belonged to it, do you submit to its rules: "Do not handle! Do not taste! Do not touch!"? These are all destined to perish with use, because they are based on human commands and teachings. Such regulations indeed have an appearance of wisdom, with their self-imposed worship, their false humility and their harsh treatment of the body, but they lack any value in restraining sensual indulgence.*
>
> (Colossians 2:20–23)

In a world of many temptations, some churches have chosen to respond by placing burdensome boundaries on their people. Indeed, asceticism (extreme self-denial, i.e. vows of poverty, celibacy, teetotaling, etc.) may *seem* like a godly path. The letter to the Colossians shows us that the early church struggled with some of the same issues that still confront us today.

In the present case, it is only right to place *some* limitations on the sale of booze. Children shouldn't buy beer, and their parents shouldn't be allowed to warm a barstool at all hours of the night. Even so, every citizen at or above the age of reason is entitled to a certain amount of personal liberty. And in the end, neither a church nor a state legislature will ever really be able to protect us from the consequences of our own bad choices.

The Blue Law, like the strict religious disciplines codified by the Pharisees or the Gnostics, may have a noble intention. It seeks to produce a more virtuous populace. But virtue, without free will, is really no virtue at all.

New Wineskins and Old

The disciples of John the Baptist did not appreciate the unique role that Jesus would play in their future. So they approached Him with a question: Why did He and His followers fail to keep some of the same customs that were observed by other Jews? (Matt. 9:14–17) It's very simple, He told them, new wine must be poured into new wineskins, not old. An old wineskin, worn from use, would likely break—and both the wine and the skins would be ruined. In other words, Jesus would be bringing them a new way of life that could not fit into the old forms.

Through the ages, and into our own present era, this advice has sometimes gone unheeded. Often, Christian missionaries in strange new lands have felt a need to "compete" for converts with the native religions. In order to make the faith more familiar and more palatable to the locals, they simply co-opted the regional customs. Out of a perceived necessity, the Gospel was blended with a wide array of centuries-old pagan beliefs and practices.

Do you know why we say "God bless you" when someone sneezes? It's because the ancient Greeks believed that your soul escapes in a sneeze.

Why do we celebrate Christmas in December? After all, we have no evidence that the early church recognized such a holiday. But the pagan festival of Saturnalia was observed during that time, in celebration of the winter solstice. What better way to attract Roman pagans to the faith than to adopt their religious customs?

In time, various elements were borrowed from Judaism, such as incense, altars, the priesthood, and the pattern of Solomon's temple with "holy" buildings and "holier" rooms. In the nations where female deities were recognized, Christian teachers countered with their own Mary as the embodiment of feminine piety and humility. Through the ages her status has risen to a level just barely short of deity. And yes, even the Easter holiday is a pagan accommodation, in honor of the goddess of fertility!

In other words, they poured old wine into new wineskins.

Special liturgies have been developed to accommodate these situations. In many cases, the meaning and origins of these copycat practices have been lost to history. Even so, in some places they have been retained as obligatory Christian observances. Becoming a Christian was *easy,* because the people didn't really have to change. They didn't need to renounce their old idolatry and superstitions. Instead, they simply held on to their old customs, overlaid with a smattering of Christian vocabulary and imagery.

Conclusion

One of these days, each of us will stand before the throne of the Almighty God, to give an account for our lives. Sound doctrine, self-control, and holy living. Mom, Dad, and Pastor Bob won't be there to intervene. You may belong to a wonderful church, but at the last trumpet that membership card and denominational creed will mean nothing. We are saved as *individuals,* not as groups.

We must re-examine why we believe as we believe, and why we do as we do. Then we must teach others and hold them accountable. This may be a difficult and challenging process, to rethink a lifetime's worth of religious training. I know it was for me, when I repented of my religious pride and became a Christian in the fall of 1990.

CHAPTER 10

beware the instant pudding!

Being spiritually lazy, we naturally tend to gravitate toward the easiest way of settling our religious questions for ourselves and others...The trouble is that the whole "accept Christ" attitude is likely to be wrong. It shows Christ applying to us rather than us to Him. It makes him stand hat-in-hand awaiting our verdict on Him, instead of our kneeling with troubled hearts awaiting His verdict on us. It may even permit us to "accept Christ" by an impulse of mind or emotions, painlessly, at no loss to our ego and no inconvenience to our usual way of life.
(A.W. Tozer, *What it Means To Accept Christ*)

My grandmother was a very sensible woman. She was quite "liberated" for a Southern belle of her generation, though she would never admit to it as such. She drove her own car, pumped her own gas, and declined every offer from a boxboy to carry her groceries. This lovely rural Texas sprite tended a garden, raised four children, and kept a busy schedule that would put many an able young man to shame.

Remember the story about how Jesus fed the five thousand with five loaves and two fishes? In no time at all, Nana could serve up a banquet to a crowd of unexpected guests out of last night's leftovers—and no one would be the wiser. And let us not forget the annual Thanksgiving dinner. This was quite a workout, especially since there always seemed to be at least one more mouth to feed each year. But she would hoist that 25-pound tom turkey in and out of the oven every time, and never break a sweat. When this precious golden poultry emerged, it was so moist and tender that you could cut it with a spoon.

In all of her 79 years she never touched a microwave oven or an automatic dishwasher. No boxed stuffing or canned cranberries allowed in Mrs. Hutson's kitchen. Wouldn't know what to do with a food processor, a garage door opener, or a disposable diaper. She did things the hard way, mostly by choice, and it wasn't because she was ignorant or couldn't afford the newfangled gadgets. Idle hands, Nana knew, are the devil's workshop; this is why she insisted to my mother that I should have household chores. (Gee, thanks...)

This attitude produces so much more than just the desired result of the moment (such as a meal). In addition, it builds personal character and a genuine sense of satisfaction.

Instant Salvation?

The innovations of our modern technology are both a blessing and a snare. They meet a legitimate need in our very busy lives, to be sure, but sometimes they also serve to cultivate the darker side of our human nature. Witness TV remote controls, supersonic flight, and pizza delivery that's free if not received within 30 minutes. Instant pudding, instant messaging, instant cameras, and Minute Rice. Instant gratification! We want it fast, we want it easy, and most of all, we want it NOW.

So what does any of this have to do with religion?

No doubt, no matter how dutiful or devoted you might be, you will always be susceptible to the same human frailties as anyone else. So if you are expecting instant results in every other area of life, then it's only natural that it *could* carry over into your relationship with God.

I know it did for me. The last time I attended a revival meeting, about 17 years ago, the minister preached a very moving sermon about the perils of instant gratification. We should not be hasty in our decision making, he told us. Teens should not rush into intimate relationships that they may regret soon afterward. True fulfillment comes from hard work, and all good things come to those who wait. Valuable words of wisdom, I thought, nodding in agreement.

...And then he invited the several hundred people in attendance to come forward and make an impulsive decision to follow Jesus and be saved.

Huh?

In our own age, many of the Christians that you know will probably attribute their redemption to some type of quick, painless experience. Maybe they "received Christ" or recited the Sinner's Prayer. The terminology varies, but the concept is the same—they received instant salvation.

A.W. Tozer, one of the great evangelists of the early 20th century, understood this syndrome. By simply "accepting Christ," it puts a sinner in the driver's seat and assumes that Christ has already accepted *you*. This approach is sometimes known, cynically, as "decisional regeneration."

Just as individual people are eager to be saved, likewise some churches are equally as impatient to see their flocks grow. For this reason, they might measure the fruitfulness of their ministries in terms of "decisions for Christ." But has Christ made a decision for *them?* The world may never know, because (in many cases) they never really asked the question.

This year, millions of people the world over will undergo this experience in various ways. It may be during a regularly scheduled worship service at a local church, or at a giant citywide revival meeting. They will hear powerful sermons by well-respected evangelists, and untold masses will walk down the aisle to confess Jesus as Lord. One by one, they will be assured that their sins are forgiven, and their souls saved.

But did your preacher happen to mention that this practice did not exist (in any organized fashion) until the early 19th century?

Yes, it's true. This popular "plan of salvation," so broadly practiced around the world, was not taught until about 200 years ago—almost *1800 years after Christ!* And even after the Sinner's Prayer arrived on the scene, it would not be widely accepted until many years later. This method can be easily discredited in three different ways: by consulting Scripture, by examining history, and by considering its practical implications.

Scripture

There is nothing in the Scriptures to commend this practice, and we search in vain for any example that Jesus or the apostles ever converted someone in this manner. In fact, there is much in the Bible—both by command and by example—to *refute* it. There are, however, a few passages that many will cite in defense of the method:

A misunderstood promise

> *Ask and it will be given to you; seek and you will find; knock and the door will be opened to you.*
> (Matthew 7:7)

Here, it appears that Jesus has promised to give us whatever we ask. So why not salvation? Can't we get forgiven simply by asking? Yes, at first glance, this conclusion might *seem* reasonable. But wait, there's more...

As we all know, the First Amendment of the U.S. Constitution guarantees us the right of free speech and a free press. Even so, the highest courts of our land have consistently held that the right is not absolute. As you go around exercising your "right," you can't publish fabricated stories to smear someone's good name. You could still be prosecuted for a crime called libel, or another called slander. And naturally, it doesn't give you the right to shout "Fire!" in a crowded theater. Still, there will always be people among us who claim First Amendment protection for the most insidious crimes. And they often find themselves on the wrong side of the scales of justice.

Likewise, the promises of God are not always absolute. Sometimes they're conditional (see chapter 6). Or the Lord will turn a deaf ear to those who ask with impure motives (James 4:3) or doubt (James 1:5–8). A blessing may be denied because the person lacks faith (Matt. 9:29), or a genuine love for God (Rom. 8:28). Matthew 7 offers a *general* promise, which describes the natural eagerness of God to shower blessings on His children. The Bible's broader teaching on salvation, on the other hand, is very *specific*.

A misconstrued prophecy

Everyone who calls upon the name of the Lord will be saved.
(Romans 10:13)

This promise is often cited as "proof" of a simple one-step plan of salvation; offering up a prayer at an altar call seems to meet this standard...doesn't it? Well, let us start at the beginning:

In Joel 2, this phrase is employed as a prophecy, to describe a future event that will take place in Jerusalem. (There's probably a cross-reference footnote in your Bible to point this out.)

In Acts 2, Peter explains that *Pentecost* was the fulfillment of Joel's prophecy. He then went on to command the people to be baptized in the name of the Lord.

In Acts 22:16, this *calling* was associated with baptism. This is also the case in many churches today; the standard liturgy for a baptism requires us to invoke the name of Jesus.

With this in mind, what shall we make of the pronouncement at Romans 10:13? As with many things in the Bible, this statement was not made in a vacuum. It was written within the context of a broader story. So let us consider the *immediately* preceding verse, and the context will become clear:

> *For there is no difference between Jew and Gentile...*(v. 12)

In other words, the Gentiles could now enjoy the blessings once reserved for the Jews. Jew and Gentile alike are under the curse of sin, and both are offered the opportunity to confess Christ and be saved. In the eyes of God, there is no longer any distinction between them. (This is one of the major themes of the book of Romans.) The opportunity to "call upon the name of the Lord" for one's salvation was now open to *everyone.*

And finally, this very approach is explicitly refuted in the words of Jesus himself at the Sermon on the Mount:

> *Not everyone who says to me, "Lord, Lord" shall enter the kingdom of heaven, but he who does the will of my Father in heaven.*
>
> (Matthew 7:21)

Talk is cheap. We all must *obey*.

Paul's conversion. In Acts 9 and 22, the experience of the mighty apostle is described in detail:

- He was given a miraculous vision from God;
- Believed in Jesus;
- Fasted from food and drink;
- Prayed for guidance; and
- Received a divine healing.

In just three short days, he witnessed more glorious things than you and I may ever hope to see in our entire lifetimes. During this period, Paul (the same person who wrote Romans 10) exhibited all of the traits and behaviors that we normally associate with piety and salvation. In fact, from the above description, it almost sounds like he answered the invitation at a revival meeting!

...But by his own account, he was not yet saved. Observe Paul's response to these events:

- Didn't try to do it by himself;
- He set aside his own existing beliefs;
- Followed his instructions (*completely,* not partially); and
- Submitted to the authority and instruction of another *human.*

All of this, of course, is quite contrary to human nature. Even more so, for a man who already fancied himself a prophet of God. But again, by his own account, Paul's conversion was still incomplete. In order to complete the process, Ananias urged him to be baptized.

Counting the cost. And finally, Jesus tells us

in no uncertain terms (Luke 14:25–33) that any decision to follow him must be an *informed* decision. For example, you wouldn't build a tower without first considering the cost of the materials, labor, and land...or would you? You wouldn't go to war without sizing up your adversary...right? Likewise, anyone who wishes to follow Jesus must take into account all of the commitments and sacrifices that it brings. This is the most important decision that you will ever make in your life, and it should not be taken lightly. An altar call which requires an immediate decision does not provide the necessary environment for this all-important process to happen.

But Didn't Peter say...?

In making the case for instant conversion, some will point to the example of Peter at Pentecost (Acts 2). Didn't he ask the people to come forward to accept Jesus? Well, I suppose you could put it that way. But it's not quite that simple.

Who was Peter speaking to? They were devout observant Jews, who had just made the long and difficult pilgrimage to Jerusalem (in many cases, hundreds of miles) to celebrate the Feast of Weeks. So they didn't need to be persuaded to follow God, or to devote themselves to His service. (Indeed, their very presence in the Holy City showed that they were already doing so.) And they didn't need to be taught how to pray, as they were already gathered for that purpose. Such a people already knew who Jesus was, and they were familiar with the messianic prophecies of the Old Testament. Further, they had just witnessed a spontaneous miracle of God, with the disciples (who normally spoke Greek) speaking in their language.

So what they needed, at this point, was for someone to connect the dots and show them that the prophet from Nazareth *was,* in fact, their long-awaited Messiah. So Peter did just that, by quoting from the prophet Joel. And when they displayed deep sorrow for their sins, he did in fact ask them to come forward—not to pray, but to repent and be baptized. (Of course, this observation alone may not disprove the validity of an altar call; but clearly, Acts 2 is not a proof text for it.)

And Didn't Jesus say…??

Here I am! I stand at the door and knock. If anyone hears my voice and opens the door, I will come in and eat with him and he with me.

(Revelation 3:20)

At first glance, to the uninitiated, this excerpt from the letter to the Laodiceans might *appear* to be conclusive proof of instant salvation through prayer. But if you're like me, when you receive a letter in the mail, you probably read the beginning first. Any other way, and there's a good chance that you won't understand the stuff in the middle—or at least not in the way that the writer intended. This would be the case if the letter were from your girlfriend, your lawyer, or from Publisher's Clearing House. In other words, *context* is crucial.

Among the books of the Bible, Revelation may be especially hard to understand. It is filled with enigmatic symbols and rich imagery. While it is not always possible to know exactly what a Bible passage means, we can sometimes be certain of what it does *not* mean. In the present case, we can know with certainty that it is *not* intended to be evangelistic. In other words, it is *not* an invitation to unbelievers. How can we be sure of this? In the very first verse of chapter 1, the book is addressed to "his (Jesus') servants." In verse 9, John describes himself as "your brother." As for the seven short letters that follow, each of them is likewise clearly addressed to an existing body of believers.

So with this in mind, let us start at the beginning of the letter, which is at chapter 3, verse 14. The message is directed to the "angel of the *church* in Laodicea." What is a church? It is a body of saved people. These individuals have no need to be invited to the altar, because they're already been converted. We know this, because the Greek word for "love" in verse 19 is *phileo* (as in *Philadelphia*), a term for brotherly love that is *never* used in the Bible when addressing a stranger. It assumes that the speaker already has a relationship with the listener.

In the middle of the 18th century, a Boston preacher named John Webb was apparently the first to use this verse in encouraging instant conversion:

> *Here is a promise of union to Christ; in these words, I will come in to him. i.e. If any sinner will but hear my voice and open the door, and receive me by faith, I will come into his soul, and unite him to me, and make him a living member of that my mystical body of which I am the Head.*
>
> (Christ's Suit to the Sinner, 14)

In other words, he completely isolated the *text* of this verse from its *con*text.

Typically (as with Paul's writings), such a letter would be read aloud before the congregation, so that everyone could hear. And as they listened to the letter being read, before reaching verse 20, they also had to get past the admonition in verse 16:

So, because you are lukewarm—neither hot nor cold—I am about to spit you out of my mouth.

Let's use a simple illustration here. Suppose that you got a letter in the mail, and it starts out with the words "I want a divorce." This must be about the most disturbing news that any man could ever hear. Twenty years together, three kids, a minivan and a mortgage, and now *this!* But then you read the name at the end of the letter, and realize...hey! That's not your wife's name! This letter was delivered to your house by mistake; it should have gone to the guy across the street. Suddenly you breathe a sigh of relief, realizing that the message in the letter doesn't apply to you.

Now let's take another look at verse 16. If Jesus is going to spit you out of His mouth (divorce you), doesn't that imply that you're already *in* His mouth (married to Him)? Yes, I agree that this is a strangely graphic analogy. But remember, Jesus said it first.

Oh yes, and it gets worse. It would appear that the editors of most modern Bible versions were just a bit timid when they translated this verse. That is, the Greek term rendered as "spit" (KJV "spew"), is actually something closer to "vomit."

The choice of this strong language is significant.

Why does a person vomit? This reflex is a natural component of your body's immune system. If you eat too much, or eat something toxic, your body will recognize it as harmful. When this poison is detected, it is expelled with great force before it can harm the rest of your body. It is an entirely involuntary response, and impossible to suppress. As unpleasant as the experience might be, it is a healing mechanism created by God.

Just as a foreign chemical or bacterium can destroy your flesh, so too can an unrepentant believer defile a congregation. He sets a poor example for others, leading them astray with his errant beliefs and immoral behavior. He is a wolf in the sheep pen, a poison in the fellowship, a cancer that must be removed with great conviction and dispatch (1 Cor. 5:1–13). This is a painful and difficult process, and in fact may end up separating friends. But it is something that must be done if the body is to survive and flourish. In the present case, the disease was much more malignant: the apostate *congregation* at Laodicea had contaminated the larger Body of Christ.

Which door? So If Jesus is knocking on a door, where exactly is said door? According to one popular teaching, it is the door of an unconverted person's heart. But from what we have just seen, this is impossible. Take a closer look, and you'll see that the picture here is of Jesus at the door of His *church*. Yes, the church! A sadder and more improbable situation can scarcely be imagined, but that is exactly what happened. The House of God became a den of iniquity, and Jesus was on the outside looking in. The Laodiceans became worldly and forgot their purpose.

Once this is understood, it becomes clear that Jesus was exhorting *Christians* (saved, forgiven church members) that they must repent of their lukewarmness and "open the door" to *remain* in a relationship with Him. This is hardly a comforting thought, and certainly not a means of initial conversion or salvation.

- A threat of divorce means nothing if it comes from a stranger.
- The thought of losing fellowship with Jesus would hold no terror for an unbeliever.
- The threatened loss of a lampstand (Rev. 2:5) would hardly motivate a person who doesn't have one, or doesn't know what it *is*.
- No writer in the world would send an encrypted message to someone who isn't "on the inside" to know what it means.

Therefore, this message would only make sense for a person who is already a saved Christian.

History

Let's suppose that you were able to convince me that an altar call is a legitimate path to salvation. Maybe my understanding of the above Scriptures is entirely wrong. If so, then I would naturally expect to find some type of evidence for it in the record of history. There would be a paper trail leading back a few hundred years, perhaps even to the time of the apostles or the church fathers. (Your other religious beliefs are well-documented; why not this one?) Any *new* invention, I think we can agree, would need to be justified in the light of Scripture.

Well, how about it?

Again, as with any teaching or practice, the history of its development is important. And just as significantly, most of its practitioners have no idea where it came from. (Do you?) Much has been reported about this record, some of which is uncertain; we will attempt to separate fact from fiction, and recount only the information that is agreed upon by most historians.

The earliest precursor of this practice appears to have been in the mid-18th century, during the Great Awakening. While the evangelists of this era sometimes encouraged their listeners to accept instant conversion, they did *not* employ altar calls or a Sinner's Prayer.

Perhaps the earliest of these teachers was Eleazar Wheelock, in the early 1740's. He would target certain people by having them sit in the front pew, which he called the "Mourner's Seat." During the sermon, he would declare that "salvation was looming over their heads." Afterward, they would be quite open to any instructions he might give. And before the meeting was over, he would proclaim them saved. Still, the practice that we now know as the altar call was yet to come.

In colonial New England, the most common practice for a Christian conversion was thus: A person would attend a worship service, feel moved in his heart, and return home to pray and struggle in private. Once a breakthrough was felt, the new convert would then repair to the minister's house to report his conversion. In time, various methods were devised to secure this commitment in a more public way.

As the pioneering settlers moved west, organized religion was difficult to, well, organize. There were no big cities, no radio or television, and no mass transportation. Very few churches were available to provide a regular, ongoing curriculum of religious instruction.

Small scattered settlements could not support a full-time minister of their own. To fill this need, they were served by a loose federation of itinerant preachers called "circuit riders." These devoted young men would travel hundreds of miles per week on horseback, serving perhaps a handful of people at each stop. Typically, it would take a month or more for a circuit rider to "make the round" to all of the stops on his route. For this reason, a given town might be served by a different preacher each Sunday, each one representing a different denominational tradition. As many as three or four preachers might share the work in that town, in a weekly rotation.

The religious landscape of this young emerging nation was in a continual state of flux. Toward the end of the eighteenth century, revival meetings were being conducted in various areas of the western frontier. The "camp meeting" form of revival became popular during this time, and these outdoor gatherings in a forest clearing would sometimes last as long as five days, attracting an audience from a radius of perhaps 50 miles or more. Whole families might pitch a tent and camp out on the grounds. This period of newfound evangelistic fervor became known as the "Second Great Awakening."

Among the earliest of these revivals, a notable hub of activity emerged at Cane Ridge, Kentucky, around 1801. Some of the most important leaders of this movement were Barton Stone and James McGready.

As many as seven sermons might be heard at once. Some were the well-planned homilies of trained ministers, while others apparently were the impromptu speeches of laymen who felt inspired by the moment. Some of these speakers were circuit riders. Tree stumps or wagons would be called into service as pulpits, in various places around the grounds. By one estimate, as many as 25,000 people would attend the meetings at a time; day and night, the sermons continued almost nonstop.

The meetings were interdenominational in scope, as clergymen from Presbyterian, Methodist, Shaker, and Baptist backgrounds joined in. The preacher would typically deliver an evangelistic message, exhorting the audience to turn their lives over to God. At the end of the discourse, those so moved would retreat into the woods, to pray and meditate in private. When the person reached a state of peace, he would return to the meeting (instead of the minister's home) to report that he had been converted. This ill-defined experience would be determined subjectively by each individual.

This arrangement evolved over time, as the speakers compared notes and experimented with various methods. Finally, a fairly standardized procedure took hold:

Toward the end of his sermon, the minister would invite his listeners to come forward to the front of the audience, and kneel at the "anxious seat." This would now be the venue for the prayer, and the assurance of the seeker's salvation. In this manner, a greater sense of order was given to the meeting, and the leaders could more readily measure how many souls were being saved. The process came to be known as the "invitation," or (later) the altar call.

At Cane Ridge, as in other places, the camp meetings encouraged instantaneous conversions. The crowds were often caught up in a frenzy; some would run around, some would shout, others would faint. According to one observer, "the noise was like the roar of Niagara." Many people experienced "the jerks"—involuntary convulsions that were attributed to the Sprit of God. The leaders actually *encouraged* this disorder, for they presumed it to be evidence of divine approval. *Emotionalism* was the order of the day, because it seemed to be so effective in bringing a steady flow of new converts.

Opposition. This message was accepted easily enough at the camp meetings, in a setting where the listeners typically had little religious training. But when the evangelists preached in the cities, they met a more sophisticated audience. The urban dwellers, typically more educated, were settled into regular routines. For many, this included frequent church attendance; the city folk already held some very strong religious convictions, and so were less receptive than those on the frontier. They were not as quick to embrace this approach, recognizing it as a recent innovation.

The New Trend Catches On

Around 1835, attorney Charles Finney experienced a profound conversion while on his knees in his office and felt a calling to preach the Gospel. Shortly afterward, he abandoned his law practice and became an evangelist in the Presbyterian tradition. Finney exported the mourner's bench to other states, preaching to thousands at a time. He wrote of this arrangement:

> *The church has always felt it necessary to have something of this kind to answer this very purpose. In the days of the apostles, baptism answered this purpose. The gospel was preached to the people, and then all those who were willing to be on the side of Christ, were called out to be baptized. It held the place that the anxious seat does now as a public manifestation of their determination to be Christians.* [13]

In other words, Finney explicitly declared that baptism—for *any* purpose—is no longer necessary!

In the 1860s, a young Dwight Moody came on the scene. He quickly recognized the folly that was inherent in the emotional outbursts and simplistic conversions. Instead of calling for a public decision under pressure, he asked people to join him and his trained counselors in a chamber called the Inquiry

Room. While this was a slight improvement, these brief private meetings typically ended with the Sinner's Prayer.

After Moody's death in 1899, R.A. Torrey revised the methodology yet again by approaching people on the streets of Chicago. Without the benefit of a sermon, he would invite them to accept Jesus "right here, right now." Whereas the revival meetings afforded a modicum of fellowship, the street conversions allowed people to go on their way very quickly.

Around this same time, Billy Sunday gained a wide following, also in the Chicago area. A former baseball player from Iowa, he forsook his sporting career and conducted large revival meetings. His flamboyant style was sometimes an asset, sometimes a liability. At times the salvation experience was connected to a prayer; at other times, people were assured of their salvation if they would only walk down the aisle (the "sawdust trail") to the altar. Many unconfirmed legends have credited him with various miraculous powers.

But the greatest exponent of this trend was still to come, in the person of Billy Graham. Beginning with a large crusade in Los Angeles in 1949, he has taken this message around the world. While his predecessors simply cast a wide net to invite individual *people* to attend, Graham popularized the trend of inviting local *churches* to take part. Over time, whereas the earlier revivalists were often viewed with skepticism, Graham's gentle manner brought a higher level of respectability.

So what kind of church promotes this "method" today? Churches of nearly every denomination, all over the world, that's who—including those who "officially" teach a plan of salvation that's entirely different. Millions of people simply have never heard of any other way.

Practical

The dangers of instant conversion are manifold and manifest. This principle is recognized even among those (i.e. Charles Spurgeon) who don't believe that baptism belongs in the salvation process. The issues include:

Group Dynamics. As everyone knows, it is very easy for a person to get swept up in the moment, in such a setting as this. Call it peer pressure. Call it the power of suggestion. The desire to conform, to fit in, is hard-wired into our psyche. Any decision that is made under these circumstances should be carefully examined.

Impulsive decision-making. When a preacher issues an altar call, there is a very real hazard that his listeners will feel compelled to make an impulsive, emotional decision, based upon a "warm fuzzy" feeling that may not last. What more, after all, could such a lightning-fast process really hope to achieve? From my own observation, I would estimate that each person spends less than three minutes with the minister or counselor at the altar. Come on, now. Let's get real. What other type of major life decision would you make so hurriedly, and with so little information? Buy a house? Quit your job? Get married? Chances are that you've probably invested more time and energy into picking out a $2.00 box of breakfast cereal at the supermarket.

Actually, my wife and I have known (and have sometimes counseled) several impatient couples that rushed to the altar in the throes of impassioned infatuation. Typically, since we live in Southern California, the venue of choice has been Las Vegas. In every case, once the wedding night was over, they quickly became disillusioned and began to have second thoughts, even talking of divorce.

Why?

They returned home and a rude awakening occurred. Suddenly, thoughts of romance and passion gave way to the unpleasant realities of laundry, utility bills, and oil changes. Yes, that nasty gremlin called "real life" appeared. They had looked forward to the joys and privileges that married life would bring, without taking time to consider its costs and responsibilities. So it is only natural, then, that the Bible often compares fellowship with God with marriage, and false religion with adultery and prostitution.

Accordingly, if your love for each other is genuine, then you'll still be in love after a few months of courtship and counseling. Likewise, if the remorse and conviction that you feel at the revival meeting are for real, then you'll still be sorrowful and convicted after a few days or weeks of study and soul-searching. In either case, if your feelings should change within that time, you'll be better off for not having taken the plunge.

This, it seems, is exactly what Jesus had in mind when he taught the Parable of the Sower (Luke 8:1–15). The seed that was sown on the rock may represent the man who answers an altar call: He heard the Word and accepted it with great eagerness, but then fell away quickly because he had no root.

Shallow convictions. As Christians we must have *deep* roots, if we are to persevere in the faith. Too many of our preachers have been busy scattering their seed on the rock, and the rest of us have been too easily impressed by the (short-term) results.

In the meantime, as we go about encouraging these simplistic conversions:

- This person may know nothing about the Bible, or even possess one.

- This person may not have repented of his sins, or even intend to, or understand that he should.

- This person may not even have a clue as to what his sins *are*.

- This person may know nothing of what God expects of him in terms of doctrine, lifestyle, or whatever.

- This person may never join up with a local church for further training and encouragement.

The promise of everlasting life was attractive enough, but in the rush to the altar, did someone tell him that that there was a cost involved? The highway to Heaven is a toll road; it can only be traveled while carrying a cross.

Overestimating results. In a stadium-sized revival where so many come forward at once, is it really possible to gauge the outcome of each person's experience? In the course of a three-minute discussion, can you tell? Frankly, there's a good chance that you'll never know, because you may never see him again. Alas, it's too late to turn back the clock now, because you just told this person that he's saved, as you go your separate ways. And this pleasant fiction allows you to issue a press release proclaiming to the outside world that thousands of people received their salvation at your meeting last night.

But maybe I'm just being too legalistic, too caught up in my own tunnel-visioned philosophy. So just for the sake of discussion, let's assume that this person *is* saved...then what? What kind of convert does this method produce? Far too often, it may create a weak, uncommitted believer who doesn't know what he believes in.

Think about it: How can he be strong if he's wearing false armor and false confidence? How can he be committed, if you didn't explain what he should commit himself *to?*

In all fairness: Yes, there are plenty of churches out there who do a fine job of follow-up with their new converts. For many, they have small-group ministries that create an intimate sense of family among the members. But if this is your intention, then why the rush to proclaim them saved? Would it not be better to take a little longer, and make sure they know what they're getting into?

The Private Revival

Apart from these public meetings, we are also told that the Sinner's Prayer is equally effective when it is done behind closed doors, in the comfort and privacy of your own home. This may be in response to an appeal from a minister on television, or upon reading a book or religious tract. Many people, after all, may have an aversion to large crowds. Or they might suffer from a genuine clinically diagnosed social *phobia,* in which case they feel entirely *unable* to come forward at a public meeting. These approaches, in part, are designed to meet such special needs.

The latest twist, as we go to press: Instant salvation offered in an Internet chat room, anonymously and painlessly. But hey, God is gracious and forgiving, so everything's gonna be okay.

Or how about an entire *online church,* with virtual fellowship? This is a growing trend. No strings attached, no accountability, no real relationships. No need to get dressed up or be on time; just log on at your convenience and view a sermon in streaming video. Enter your credit card number once a week, and you can "tithe" to the phantom ministry.

But once again we find ourselves in conflict with the Scriptures, both by command and by example. In the early church, there was no such thing as a "solo" Christian. As we read the many conversion accounts in Acts, we find that every new convert was taught–in person–by another person. Upon their conversion, they typically became a member of a local congregation.

Consider:

- **John 13:34**—"A new command I give you: Love one another."
- **Romans 12:10**—"Be devoted to one another in brotherly love."
- **1 Corinthians 16:20**—"Greet one another with a holy kiss."
- **Hebrews 3:13**—"Encourage one another daily"

These commands of God *cannot* be fulfilled by a person who sits alone at home. It requires us to be an active part of a fellowship of like-minded believers.

The work of the ministry was conducted mainly in small groups. One-on-one instruction was very common as well, and in this type of setting, there were no large crowds to be afraid of. Even Paul, though converted through a non-routine miraculous vision from God, was nonetheless instructed to submit to another *human* (Ananias) for further instruction. This was also the pattern among the Jews of the Old Testament—no one had to go it alone.

Accountability. This do-it-yourself approach may be perfectly fitting, of course, because in recent decades people of all faiths have increasingly considered their religion to be a private matter between themselves and God. They are believers-but-not-belongers, and have little or no interest in "organized religion." After all, such an affiliation brings with it such responsibilities (read: *burdens*) as fellowship, submission, and accountability.

They find it strange, even cultic, to observe that other believers confess their sins—ritualistically and anonymously—before a clergyman in a darkened chamber. And yet they themselves routinely attend revival meetings where they can come clean before a stranger who they may never see again.

Here, you can have your conscience cleansed (momentarily) by fulfilling a legalistic duty, checking off one more item on your to-do list. There's a certain odd comfort that arises from confessing in the presence of someone who will never ask whether you actually repented of the sins confessed in the last meeting. In the meantime, your close Christian friends—the very people who care about you the most—may never know your struggles or be able to help you through them.

The Hazards of Camp Meetings

A circuit rider, on average, would ordinarily preach to fewer than a dozen people at a time. But at a camp meeting he could reach *thousands,* and all in one place. This awesome opportunity, however, also presented an unaccustomed dilemma: *How shall we deal with these eager listeners once we have their rapt attention?* Surely, it was not possible to engage in any substantial Bible study or extended discussion with each person. But on the other hand, it would be a shame to send them away unfulfilled. What to do? The invitation provided a quick, simple device to give these listeners the assurance from God that they so desperately wanted.

In short, the Altar Call and the Sinner's Prayer

are very modern innovations. They have no basis in the teaching of Jesus or the apostles, no matter how much we attempt to put words in their mouths.

These practices were entirely unknown to the Church Fathers, or the great thinkers of the Reformation, the Great Awakening, or any other religious movement prior to the 19th century. The preachers didn't need to defend their traditions by appealing to the Bible, because the people didn't know the difference.

In the meantime, while rejoicing over these new fruits of our ministry, we fail to recognize that we may have simultaneously proclaimed salvation upon hordes of unregenerate people. Surely, this approach continues to add plenty of names to our membership rosters, that we might celebrate the incredible growth.

But are their names written in the Book of Life?

Challenges of Frontier Evangelism

When Father Junipero Serra led his humble band of friars to build missions along the California coast, they had a plan. Each mission would evangelize its local area. Each, in time, was subdivided into archdiocese and diocese and parish. The belief system was firmly established, a well-planned course of instruction was in place, and everyone knew who was in charge. This systematic process served them well, and the fruits of their labors are still apparent today.

American Protestantism, however, began in the East and was built very differently. Driven westward by a sense of manifest destiny, much of our nation's population was constantly on the move. This was a time of great religious confusion, when stable church institutions were rare and experienced Bible teachers were few. In some cases, European churches refused to send bishops to serve their expatriates across the sea. So the people were largely left to start from scratch, and for the most part were in no hurry to do so. Unlike the Catholics, they had little structure, stability, or accountability.

Under the circumstances, then, perhaps this was the best they could do. So the circuit riders gladly took advantage of every opportunity to preach, even in this imperfect setting. But this doesn't mean that we should follow their pattern today. Bibles and churches are readily available for anyone who is truly searching.

The Fine Print (My Lawyers Made Me Do This)

Having discredited the only route to salvation that many people have ever known, these "disclaimers" now appear necessary:

Divine Prerogative. Is it *impossible* for someone to be saved this way? Surely not, for our God is bigger than any of our doctrinal arguments. He is fully able to gaze into each person's deepest thoughts and attitudes with surgical accuracy and determine whose hearts are truly his, without the aid of any particular ceremony—baptism, altar call, or any other. His discernment is infinitely greater than yours or mine.

Ministers. How should we regard the preachers at the camp meetings? Shall we accuse them of wholesale fraud and deception? Must we question their motives and intentions? No, I will not attempt to speculate as to what's going on inside another man's head. And I take no pleasure in *ad hominem* character assassination, because it proves nothing.

But as we have seen, many of these clergymen represented denominations with a known body of belief. Some already recognized Wesley's *Treatise on Baptism,* written less than 50 years earlier, within the lifetime of some of the participants. Others subscribed to Knox's *Scottish Confession* or the Nicene Creed. All of these documents, of course, require a much different process for conversion. In other words, whatever their motivations, *they knew better*.

Audience. Again, as with the preachers, I will never question the sincerity or devotion of a person who answers an altar call. I'm perfectly willing to admit that every person has the best of intentions.

Likewise, I dare not question any person's *experience*. You say that you felt the overwhelming presence of God at the altar? Great. No doubt, our God makes himself known to us in any number of ways. You say that your life changed from that day forward? Wonderful. To be sure, there are far too many believers out there who never manage to meet their maker on such a tangible, visceral level.

But again, that's not the point.

In spite of what you might have heard, or felt, or experienced, there *is* a normative way of salvation.

The apostles taught a very specific plan, and *that* is the one that we should be teaching to our people. And *obeying,* both as institutions and as individuals. So again, yes, there may be exceptions. But in many churches, and in many stadium-size revival meetings, it seems as if *everyone* is the exception!

To be clear: I *do not* believe that most people actually make a conscious, deliberate decision to walk this lonely road. Even so, it is the natural outgrowth of many modern trends. Believers today would prefer to blaze new trails, where the roads have no rules. It's progressive, it's hip, it's cutting edge, it's *now*. Absolute truth is a thing of the past, and personal experience is everything.

A Closer Look

The leaders of your own local church may conduct an altar call at the end of every worship service, urging people to "receive Christ." They might teach the Sinner's Prayer to every lost soul who comes forward, perhaps thousands each year. Baptism may be barely a symbolic gesture reserved for those who wish to dedicate their children or become members of the flock. Scores of delegates might be sent off to every revival meeting that rolls through town.

But tucked away somewhere in the bottom drawer of a dusty old filing cabinet, in the deepest, darkest recesses of the church basement, there may lie a creed or confession that no one talks about. (That is, the document without which your church might not exist!) And it instructs the church to baptize people *for the remission of their sins.*

But you could be a member for many years and never know this important part of their "official" doctrine, based upon the sermons that are preached from the pulpit.

When the congregation was established 50 or 80 or 100 years ago, every member or prospective convert was expected to study the confession and know what they believed in. And they did. Their denominational affiliation was not just a name on the letterhead, or a sign on the building, but a meaningful declaration to the world as to who they were and what they stood for. Methodists knew why they were Methodists, and Baptists knew why they were Baptists.

And what about us today, who gladly claim this noble ancestry? For many of us, we don't even know the difference, or recognize that there's a problem.

Sooo…You Got a Better Idea?

Sometimes it's easy to think of "church" as a corporate entity driven by programs, liturgies, and rules. We have a plan, we have a process, and no doubt people often respond. We long to tell them x, y, and z; we've been doing it this way for a hundred years, and it works, by golly. But is this what *this* person needs at *this* moment? Maybe he needs to be assured that it's okay to have doubts. Or maybe she needs to learn how to cope with raising three children as a single mother. Do we know? Did we ask? Or are we only concerned with following a pre-written recipe?

Short of offering instant salvation, there are many things that we can do to welcome our visitors into the fellowship. Start up a weekly new believers' class, if you don't already have one. Take them out to lunch or dinner after church, pick up the check, and exchange phone numbers. Invite them into your home, and let your kids play together. Set up a time for personal Bible study over tea and scones, and then answer their questions. Share from your own life and confess your own sins and struggles. In the Bible, in both testaments, *hospitality* is commended as a noble virtue. When Priscilla and Aquila trained the young evangelist Apollos (Acts 18), they did so together, and *in their home.*

Have a church picnic in a public park, and invite your friends and neighbors to attend. Set out the fatted calf and play volleyball or baseball. Many people, when approached in this informal setting away from crosses and choir lofts, may well be open to spiritual discussions—especially when you feed them. Let them observe the intimate fellowship among your members; maybe this is what they are looking for, even if they don't know it yet. Then the conversation is no longer a boring college lecture, but a friendly chat between friends. They start to know you, perhaps even like you. And then they'll trust you to teach them.

Get the rank-and-file members involved, and they may end up doing most of the work. If you put them in charge of teaching others, they will be challenged to sharpen their own skills. The ministry staff can then be freed up to oversee the process, and provide back-up support when the tough questions arise. When your members feel like their contributions are valued in the ministry, they tend to stick around year after year. Likewise, when the newcomer finally makes his decision to become a Christian, he will have a firmer foundation for his newfound faith. When doubts arise (and they surely will), he will have a built-in support system to fall back on.

Which, of course, brings us back to my original thesis statement in the introduction: Do your people have the knowledge and wisdom to do this? Are they well trained in the Scriptures and in your church doctrines? Can they take a first-time visitor by the hand and train him through to the point that he's ready to confess Christ and be saved?

Anyone can get them to come forward and recite a prayer. But where will they be a year from now? This is the key to any successful evangelistic enterprise.

CHAPTER 11

the legacy of the reformation

When an evil spirit comes out of a man, it goes through arid places seeking rest and does not find it. Then it says, "I will return to the house I left"...Then it goes and takes seven other spirits more wicked than itself, and they go in and live there. And the final condition of that man is worse than the first.
(Luke 11:24–26)

b e careful what you pray for. You just might get it.

In recent years, all over the world, malevolent dictators have fallen from power in spectacular ways. Saddam Hussein in Iraq, Slobodan Milosevic in Yugoslavia, and Nicolae Ceausescu in Romania, just to name a few. This is always a joyous occasion for the citizens of a country, as they dance in the streets to celebrate their liberation.

But then morning comes, bringing with it the inexorable national hangover. They gather the empty champagne bottles, sweep up the confetti, and swallow hard. And they are faced with a daunting question: *Now what?* Will their next ruler actually be an improvement over the last? It's one thing to lead an opposition movement, quite another to actually *govern*. Will their lives actually change for the better? Too early to tell. Still, in desperation, they take their chances.

In the same way, Jesus once told a story about an evil spirit that came out of a man. This demon went about trying to find rest, but when it could find none it returned to from whence it came, along with seven others. So the final condition of the man was worse than before. Why? Because the man had not sought to fill that same space with something else—namely, the Spirit of God. Such has been the case with a great many political and religious movements over the years, and the Reformation—the 16th century religious upheaval in Europe, which attempted to purify the church of the many false teachings and practices promulgated by Rome—was no exception.

Out of the Frying Pan...

To be sure, many of us are happy to claim the Reformation-era teachers as our religious ancestors. Here was the situation: The authority of God was seen as coming from the human leaders of the church, and clergymen claimed the authority to forgive sins. The power of religion was attributed to the many rituals, and an increasingly formalized liturgy. Divine grace was doled out selectively as a commodity, as so many soybeans. Imperial influence forced the church to sell its soul for thirty pieces of silver, and many wealthy patrons were all too eager to buy. The ever-evolving, ever-more-complicated *institution,* originally intended as a channel to God, in time became an object of devotion unto itself.

Over time, corruption was rooted out; idolatry was exposed; the Scriptures gained a new level of respect. Indeed, in many cases, this reform was a *good* thing as many significant errors were brought to light and corrected. Evil spirits (like unjust rulers) were cast out, indeed. But what, exactly, would take their place?

...Into The Fire

Finally, let us recognize what the Reformation did *not* achieve. What was the original problem that made it necessary? No doubt, the individual issues were many, and each situation was unique. Ultimately, however, the root cause was the exaltation of men, tradition, and creeds. After all was said and done, how did the story end?

If we examine the various new church bodies that emerged from this turbulent era, we will find that they still—to this day—greatly resemble the society from whence they came. Church and state remain tightly bound in many places, and the wealthy are granted special favors. Denominations, local congregations, and ecumenical ministries are named in honor of mortal men. Creeds abound; Original Sin and infant baptism remain. Tradition and ritual still prevail. Someone else (parents, friends, clergyman, etc.) has already done all the thinking for us, so all we have to do is trust them to tell us what to do and what to think and what to believe.

In other words, in many places, whether we

choose to admit it or not, our religion is now rooted in *different* men, *different* traditions, and *different* creeds. All of this is terribly ironic, of course, because we moderns actually *have* the education and the printing technology that were not available to our brethren of as little as 200 years ago. Bibles can be found in hotel rooms, public libraries, even at Kmart! So there's really no excuse for someone like you or me.

Which is not to say that we haven't made a great deal of progress. In most places, kings and presidents now rule the state, but not the church. Bishops rule the church, but not the state. We might worship in a bungalow or under a tree instead of requiring a fancy cathedral. We feel free to think for ourselves and question the old ways. The minister may wear denim jeans and sneakers, and not a robe of many colors. He might preach from a modern-language Bible. We may be less dogmatic, and more inclusive. Without a doubt, we have come a long way from the errors and idolatries of yesteryear.

Still, in many of these same places, the story remains the same. We reject one man-made confession, embrace the next, and fail to read our Bibles. We continue in the indiscriminate baptizing of unbelievers, and just as quickly lose track of them. We disown one superhuman teacher only to exalt another, and then just long enough to discover that he, too, has feet of clay. One set of man-made traditions is exchanged for a "better" one. Clergymen travel far and wide to meddle in politics, while neglecting their flocks. Likewise, political leaders are granted the use of church pulpits to campaign for public office. So in the end, we remain devoted to *men* and *traditions* and *creeds*. And of course, we are now more religiously divided and confused than at any time in our history. Movements and philosophies come and go as swiftly as ever, but human nature will never change.

Sometimes, in the effort to reform the church, the cure was not much better than the disease itself. The reformers won some very important and strategic battles, but they lost the war.

An Illustration

Suppose that you had a pet dog, but you'd really prefer to have a cat. But there was only one pet store in town, and they only sold dogs. What to do? If you were really determined, you could (in theory) have your pet surgically altered to resemble a cat. Give him pointy ears, a sandpaper tongue, and retractable claws. He could be taught to "meow" instead of "woof." Feed him Cat Chow, give him a ball of yarn to play with, and the conversion would be complete.

Or would it?

At a time like this, as much as you might enjoy the illusion, we must face some hard facts. Fido, in the end, will never really cease to be a dog. He will still have doggy DNA and doggy instincts. He will still prefer kibble to catnip. And in perhaps the most telltale symptom of all, he will never stop chasing cats.

The Illustration Explained

Toward the beginning of the 16th century, the folly of the old ways was becoming apparent to many people. They longed to have an alternative, but there was only one church in town—which offered but one brand of religion. By almost all accounts, the Bride of Christ was seriously ill. Something had to be done. But who could summon the courage to resist Rome?

The great reformers, notwithstanding their many worthy contributions, were essentially closet Catholics. After all, few in Western Europe could know that any other Christian discipline even *existed*. In an age before jet travel and mass communication, it was quite rare for the average believer to ever encounter a person of another religion. So he rarely had to defend or question his own. Thus, the pioneers were just as much a product of their culture as anyone else. Luther applied his scalpel here, Calvin there, and so on. They performed surgery on a sick institution and the outward appearance of the religion did, in fact, change. But the basic genetic makeup remained the same, because Catholic doctrine continued to be the *starting point* for the alternative systems that followed. The operation excised *some* demons, while leaving others in place; so the patient was never truly healed.

Contrary to a popular misconception, then, the Reformation was **not** really a blanket renunciation of Catholic teaching. Fido, in the end, remained a dog.

Misunderstandings and Overreactions

> *But everyone who hears these words of mine and does not put them into practice is like a foolish man who built his house on sand. The rain came down, the streams rose, and the winds blew and beat against that house, and it fell with a great crash.*
>
> (Matthew 7:26–27)

This proliferation of churches and creeds is understandable, as is the peoples' rush to join them. For if you've lived long enough under an unjust ruler—or an abusive husband—or an untenable religious system—then just about any alternative will seem to be an improvement and every suitor a savior.

As we have seen, the church of the 16th century was badly in need of reform. The existing leaders had shown themselves to be poor stewards of the Good News, and it was only a matter of time until the long-simmering discontent would boil over into the public square. Few honest students of church history would disagree with this estimation. But what would be the remedy?

In many quarters this well-intended quest for the true faith has caused us to migrate, slowly but surely, from one extreme to another. That is, we once uniformly believed that rituals were *everything*, and all-powerful. Today, almost five centuries later, many of us who claim the Reformation heritage believe that ceremonies are *nothing*, and strictly symbolic.

But this brings us no closer to the truth.

Just as a foolish man builds his house (a belief

system) upon the sand, likewise an equally foolish man *buys* the house (accepts the system). It's so much easier than building from scratch. *I can just apply a fresh coat of paint* (correct a few flaws), he thinks, failing to recognize the dangers of the smaller cracks. And he has no idea how deep the sand really is.

Following this upheaval, many people felt liberated from the pomp and legalism of the old order. Indeed, men such as Luther and Calvin must be appreciated for their courage in calling for change from within a social and religious milieu that discouraged independent thinking. Time and again they risked their careers, their reputations, even their very lives, in an ongoing quest to defend the genuine Gospel.

Still, they fell short of restoring true Christianity, as defined by the primitive church. (And shouldn't this be *our* standard as well?) For every false teaching or practice that was corrected, another went unchecked. Many new ideas were introduced which were not necessarily an improvement over the old, because much of the old hyper-ceremonialism remained. Such is the hazard of patchwork reform.

Many of us, sadly, have thrown out the baby with the bathwater. Over the course of time, just about everything that Rome ever taught was re-thought and re-examined with a skeptical eye. Gradually, every word of the Catechism became suspect, and many people began to assume that everything they learned at church in their youth was a pack of lies.

But again, *this brings us no closer to the truth.*

The Roman church, to be sure, had strayed a long way from the pure and simple teaching of its apostolic ancestors. Knowing this, do you *really* want to separate fact from fiction? If so, then we must stop thinking in the divisive, parochial terms of *us* and *them*. We must ask ourselves, not *who* is right, but rather *what* is right.

Because at the end of the day, that's what really matters.

CHAPTER 12
how did we get here?
(the roots of division)

> *Make every effort to keep the unity of the Spirit through the bond of peace. There is one body and one spirit—just as you were called to one hope when you were called—One Lord, one faith, one baptism...*
> (Ephesians 4:3–5)

Very early in my research for this book, surfing the 'net at the library, I discovered that there are—literally—*thousands* of religions out there. Oh, I don't mean Judaism, Hinduism, Shinto, Buddhism, Islam, or anything like that. Rather (can you believe it?), there are thousands of *Christian* religions, which seemed to have very little in common. In fact, according to the latest edition of the World Christian Encyclopedia,[14] there are 33,820 distinct, identifiable Christian denominations in the world today.

Wow.

So how did we get here? And if the Gospel message is so simple, then how did we end up with such a wide array of views and opinions? In order to truly grasp the significance of this phenomenon, it is helpful if we examine our past. Then the "evolution" of our Christian beliefs will become clear.

Foreseen by God

We should not marvel at the present situation, for this falling away did not just *happen*. It was foretold by God from the earliest days of the church. False teachers and dividers would surely come, some from within and some from without:

> *For false Christs and **false prophets** will appear and perform great signs and miracles to deceive even the elect—if that were possible.*
>
> (Matthew 24:24)
>
> *I know that after I leave, **savage wolves** will come in among you and will not spare the flock. Even from your own number men will arise and distort the truth in order to draw away disciples after them.*
>
> (Acts 20:29–30)

To listen to some of our preachers today, it would seem as if these words of divine prophecy had never been written! They are so eager to remain in the good graces of other churches, that they have accepted the ecumenical idea that there is no such thing as a false prophet or a false teaching. "You believe what you want to believe, I believe what I want to believe, and we'll all go to heaven together." They are crying "peace, peace" when there is no peace (Jer. 8:11).

Before we can save the world, maybe we need to save ourselves first.

It Has Always Been This Way

Do you find it disturbing to hear such a dreary assessment of our modern-day religious world? Actually, an unbiased, dispassionate study of history will show us that this is exactly what has happened. If we but heed the lessons of our spiritual forebears, we will understand that this drifting from the truth is nothing new.

- Aaron made a golden calf when Moses took too long to return from the mountain, and *God's Chosen People* accepted it as a genuine object of devotion.
- In the days of the divided kingdom, only two of the twelve tribes (Judah and Benjamin) remained true to the Lord.
- In the lifetime of Elijah, nearly the entire nation of Israel forsook the Lord and worshipped idols. Only 7,000 true believers remained.
- The Messiah himself was betrayed by two of his closest friends, even after they had seen him walk on water and raise the dead.
- In the early days of the church in Jerusalem, the Gentile believers were treated as second-class citizens in a mostly-Hebrew congregation.

It happened to Moses. And Elijah. And Jesus. And the apostles. These sinful attitudes have been present from the very beginning, and they have always served to divide and corrupt the flock.

Let us not be so naïve as to assume that it can't happen to us.

Root #1: The Cumulative Effect of Small Changes

As a child, one of my favorite pastimes was a game called "Telephone," and it went something like this: Ten kids would sit in a straight line, and the first would whisper a long sentence into the ear of his neighbor. That child would then repeat the message (to the best of his memory) to the next in line, and so on. At the end of the line, the last one would announce the message to the group, as he understood it. Invariably, it would bear very little resemblance to the original. This was always good for a laugh, and we would do it over and over again until my mother called me home for supper.

Many religious doctrines have come about in this manner, cart-before-the-horse as it were, forcing apologists to crystallize new teachings on the run to keep up with events as they unfold.

In some cases, this takes the form of circular reasoning. Basically, this means that you use one unproven assumption to "prove" the next. You start with a desired conclusion, and then work backwards to build a case for it. And in this way, new teachings are sometimes built one atop the other.

A meaningless diversion? Well, yes, on one level. But this also demonstrates the way that many of our religious traditions have been handed down to us over the course of the past twenty centuries. With each passing generation, a handful of changes are made, some large and some small. Creeds and catechisms proliferated, while Bibles remained the private property of a fortunate few. Each successive teacher may truly believe that he is faithfully passing down the message, or even *improving* on it by correcting the errors of his predecessors. But over time, the cumulative effect of these changes has been *huge*.

For example:

Step 1: If we're baptizing sinless babies, it must mean they're *born* sinful.

Step 2: If they're sinful without sinning, then it *must* have been inherited from Adam.

Step 3: If this innate depravity is passed from father to son, there *must* be something evil about the procreation process.

Step 4: So the only truly spiritual people are those who abstain from all intimate relations.

You get the idea.

If you accept Step One, then Step Two seems reasonable. And so on. One small compromise begets another, which begets another. Finally, a church leader imparts his approval and the issue is settled. In time, we forget the truth entirely. All of this makes perfect sense, if you're following a religious system that holds a misguided understanding of the nature and grace of God.

When playing "Telephone," therefore, who is the more reliable expositor of the original message–the second child in the lineup, or the tenth? Obviously, it's the second. This is why the writings of the Church Fathers are so important. Irenaeus was a student of the mighty Polycarp, who in turn had been taught by the apostle John. Clement of Rome is believed to have been an associate of both Peter and Paul. With such influences, these men are in a much better position to understand the minds of the apostles—and, in turn, the mind of Christ. And *this* is no child's play.

Root #2: Heroes

In becoming a Christian, we each have our own issues to deal with. We each have our particular set of questions and struggles, strengths and weaknesses. This is a necessary part of the process, as difficult as it may be, and no one else can do it for us. But no one can do it alone.

So we look to other people to help us, which is only natural because this is exactly what God intended. (The abundance of "one-another" passages in the New Testament will testify to this). That's why he gave us a *church,* to serve as the environment for this process to happen. Even so, sometimes our dependence on a particular teacher can get out of hand, and our devotion is misplaced. Paul understood this weakness of human nature, and warned the Corinthians to keep their perspective:

> *What, after all, is Apollos? And what is Paul? Only servants, through whom you came to believe...So neither he who plants nor he who waters is anything, but only God, who makes things grow.*
>
> (1 Corinthians 3:5–7)

The preacher is the *medium,* not the *message.* He might very well be a messenger of God, and his message faultless. Still, he remains a sinful, fallible man who can make mistakes. Within an existing institution, a dissident group may rally around an engaging leader with a powerful message. In time, this group may leave to form a new church.

Root #3: Confessions Galore

All through history, men have attempted to find religious wisdom in various places. Dozens of creeds and confessions were produced, many of which are cited in these pages. The people were so hungry for answers that they devoured any writings that seemed to provide them. One consequence of this effort was that the partisans of each teacher took them a little too seriously. They divided into a plethora of denominations, creating one division after another. Accordingly, these documents have been crystallized into a new type of canon—and many of us have accepted their authority without question.

Hidden dangers. No doubt, these documents were created with the noblest of intentions. There is much wisdom to be found in them. But we must be mindful that they are not inspired Scripture, and were sometimes influenced by the political pressures of their day.

Often, our churches and seminaries will consult the writings of these reformers as a standard by which to measure the Bible. But if we really embrace this idea of *sola scriptura* (and most of us *claim* that we do), then...well, shouldn't it be the other way around?

So why do we have so many denominations?

Largely, it is because of the misplaced loyalty that is described here. (See also the comments on 1 Cor. 1, in chapter 2.)

This phenomenon still occurs today. You can probably name a few examples.

Root #4: Government Influence

From the earliest of times, governments have meddled in church affairs:

- The Council of Nicea (4th century) was initiated by Constantine.

- In many places, church and state became one. In one instance, the Church directly ruled a large area of Italy from 754 to1870 AD (the "Papal States").

- Kings appointed bishops, and bishops appointed kings. Charlemagne, for one, was appointed as Emperor on Christmas Day in 800 AD, by Pope Leo III.

- Imperialist wars were rationalized as opportunities for evangelism, or to silence heretics. During the Crusades (1095–1270 AD), millions of people were brutally killed in defense of the "true faith."

Under these circumstances, when a false teaching can be punished as a crime against the state, it should come as no surprise that our Christian doctrine has been so profoundly compromised.

Root #5: Artificial Barriers

Do you know what a "One-Cup" church is? It's a church that celebrates Communion by passing a single cup of wine (or other similar juice) to all of the congregants. They do this to emulate Jesus at the Last Supper, who passed a single cup to all of the participants.

Do you know what a foot washing ceremony is? Again, following the example of Our Lord, it is a regular practice where the members of a church wash each other's feet as part of their worship. In some places it is held up as an indispensable ordinance, on the same level as baptism and Communion.

Some churches handle snakes as a standard part of the liturgy. Others require all women to wear ankle-length dresses, or refuse to allow musical instruments. And they openly cast doubt upon the faithfulness of anyone who doesn't share the same vision, because they can't imagine worshipping God any other way.

Up north, they believe that hysterical laughter is the unmistakable sign of God's blessing. Down south, it's uncontrollable convulsions and weeping. And just about everywhere else, someone knows exactly how and when the world will end.

Do these beliefs and practices have a basis in Scripture? Sure they do, *in the proper context*. But as these people single out a particular pet issue and invent new rules—and effect a new schism along the way—they may in fact be neglecting some *other* important part of the Gospel.

Shall we go on? Home schooling, vows of silence, Sabbath observance, or a wholesale rejection of all television and movies. Pick one, or all. We consider people holier or closer to God if they are slain in the

Spirit or bear the stigmata. On a number of occasions, I have had my religions devotion called into question because I don't have a picture of Jesus in my home or a fish decal on back of my car.

I would never wish to discourage a fellow believer from doing any of these things, if they felt led to do so. But why should they be so important, so as to condemn one church and start up another? I know many people who share this mindset, protected from the evil outside world by their many rules. Such a man leads a burdened joyless existence, continually trying to prove himself worthy. He would never think of joining a monastery, and yet continues to live year after year in a cloister of his own making, where there is no room for sinners and tax collectors.

Often, when churches pile up rules upon rules, they end up preaching a burdensome gospel. No sooner is the soul freed from sin, than the nose is pressed to the grindstone. *You must do this! You can't do that!* This kind of church may never grow beyond a core group of "true believers," or have a meaningful impact on its surrounding community.

In the early church—even under the noses of the apostles—many people attempted to impose artificial "tests" of spirituality. They included:

- Circumcision (Acts 15:1)
- Sabbath observance (Col. 2:16)
- New moon festival (Col. 2:16)
- Food restrictions (Rom. 14:1)

- Hebrew ancestry (Acts 6:1)

But the Scriptures continually assure us that such regulations are not binding upon a saved Christian. All of these things are permissible, but none are required by God.

Paul, once the most strident legalist of all, had something to say about this:

> *It is for freedom that Christ has set us free. Stand firm, then, and do not let yourselves be burdened again by a yoke of slavery. Mark my words! I, Paul, tell you that if you let yourselves be circumcised, Christ will be of no value to you at all.*
>
> (Galatians 5:1–2)

In other words, Jesus died to free us from religious burdens, because experience has shown that they don't necessarily produce holier people. Yet many of us insist on taking up *new* ones, and imposing them on others.

Again, no doubt, some people find great fulfillment in observing the old customs, because it helps them feel closer to God. And they should be encouraged to continue. But as we have seen (in chapter 9), overblown traditions and hang-ups can create new walls that separate us from one another. We could learn from them, and they could learn from us. Such artificial barriers keep us isolated from people with *different* gifts and *different* insights. This is tragic because every person's contribution is important, if the church is ever going to achieve the purposes of God (1 Cor. 12).

☦

CHAPTER 13
the cost of division

> *You are all sons of God through faith in Christ...There is neither Jew nor Greek, slave nor free, male nor female, for you are all one in Christ Jesus.*
> (Galatians 3:26–28)

At its inception, our nation was envisioned as a civilization blessed by God, where all men are created equal. At long last, we were free from royal tyranny. Free from religious oppression and a social caste system that sealed a man's fate from birth. Freed, even, from a punitive tax on our afternoon cup of tea. And still it is painfully self-evident, 230 years later, that such an ideal has not been fully realized. We have the right to vote and choose our political leaders—but for a variety of reasons, the majority of us don't bother. We can know God's will by reading a Bible—but instead, many of us just follow a fixed religious system and trust someone else to study it for us. In the "Land of the Free and the Home of the Brave," a place of endless possibilities, we often settle for the path of least resistance, a life of surrender to blissful mediocrity.

Certainly God has kept his part of the bargain;

he *made* us equal, and made us free. But we as sinful men seem to have this strange way of dividing ourselves into artificial categories according to various socioeconomic criteria—rich and poor, black and white, educated and uneducated, young and old. Children learn this system at a very young age and carry it all through their lives, often never realizing that they've actually made a choice. This takes place even in melting-pot cities like New York or Los Angeles, where all of these groups can be found to reside within a ten-minute drive of each other. Why is this happening?

Nothing New

Division among Christians has been commonplace since the earliest of times. Some are even recorded in the Scriptures, and it is never characterized as a good thing. None of them, however, comes close to the scale or significance of the "Great Schism," the eleventh century rift between East (Orthodox) and West (Catholic). For almost as long, Christians have longed for the Church to be re-united into a single body as it once was. Preachers have preached, armies have marched, and kings have proclaimed, in pursuit of this wonderful ideal. (Paul wrote to the *church* in Corinth, a single institution which was unified under a common leadership and body of doctrine. Why should there now be church*es?*)

But this distress is not shared by all, for how can you possibly *miss* something you've never *had?* Out of a desire to be "open-minded," we are taught to embrace a laissez-faire attitude. We all believe in Jesus, and we all read from the same Bible. We worship the same God, so it doesn't really matter what you believe, right? One church is just as good as another, just a matter of personal preference. Or at least, that's what we would like to believe. But the consequences of this division, and of the choices we make, are enormous.

Cost #1: Confusion

During and after the Reformation, many people felt liberated to think for themselves. Their eyes were opened, and for the first time they began to consider that the old system might not hold all of the answers. This is the *good* news. At the same time, new theologies were being minted at a fast and furious pace. The people begged for answers, and the churches genuinely attempted to provide them. And the new sects multiplied.

So how are we doing *now?*

Just take a look in the Yellow Pages directory in any large American city. Look between "Chiropractors" and "Cigars." What will you find? There will be a dizzying collection of listings for "Churches." *Hundreds* of them, mostly Christian congregations. This makes it so very hard for the average seeker to find a home.

So the first fruit of sectarian division is that the people—when faced with so many choices—are utterly confused. And this perplexity is multiplied further when individual congregations affiliate themselves with more than one denomination![15]

No consistent message. No solid ground to stand on. This is the *bad* news.

Cost #2: Racial Separation

I have a dream that one day, my four little children will live in a world where they will be judged not by the color of their skin, but by the content of their character.
(Dr. Martin Luther King, Jr., 1966)

During the civil rights movement of the 1950s and '60s, people marched in the streets for social justice. They organized sit-ins, boycotts, and press conferences. As a result, we integrated our city transit buses. Restaurants, bathrooms, and water fountains were open to all. Schools and neighborhoods and workplaces became more diversified than ever. To this day we struggle with school busing and Affirmative Action, trying to find the right balance. Finally, our society is at least attempting to treat all of its citizens alike, and in some very visible ways. Hallelujah!

And yet, 40 years after this famous speech on the Capitol Mall in Washington, Dr. King's idealized colorblind society has not materialized. Sunday, he once observed, remains the most segregated day of the week.

Excuse me?

Hold the Hosannas.

Yes, this race-and class-consciousness has found its way into our religion as well. This is hard to ignore, as it often appears in the *name* of the denomination. In my old neighborhood, there is a *Japanese* Methodist Church, a *Ukrainian* Orthodox Church, and a *Polish* Catholic Church. Across town you will find the *African* Methodist Episcopal Church and the *Hungarian* Reformed Church.

And in this day and age, would you believe that we even have *white supremacist* "Christian" churches?

Yep. It's true.

Some would insist that such separation is necessary, because our cultural differences lead to varying styles of worship. I wouldn't be "comfortable" in your church, and you wouldn't be "comfortable" in mine. You sing the traditional European hymns, we sing the old Negro spirituals, and our neighbors down the street worship in a whole different language. You clap and shout, we kneel and pray. And so on. We can be friends, but hey, let's not get *too* close.

In a bygone era this division was excusable, perhaps even necessary. Many former slaves were not welcome in the "white" churches, and were forced to establish their own houses of worship. In other cases, large groups of immigrants—lost in a strange new country—banded together in their own ethnic communities. They needed to have a church where people spoke their language and understood their culture.

No doubt, we are a land of immigrants. Our nation is truly blessed because of this fascinating patchwork of cultures. But today, most of us are a few generations removed from that initial culture shock, and English is our first language. No matter where we came from, we eventually develop a taste for baseball, hot dogs, and apple pie. Just about every other institution of our American civilization is racially integrated. The job is not complete, but we have made a great deal of progress by recognizing the problem. In our own day, therefore, this Sunday morning separation is harder to justify.

Why are we gathering in the first place? We're here to worship Jesus. When he drove the moneychangers from the Temple, he declared that it should be "a house of prayer for all nations." When a subtle racism emerged in the Jerusalem church, the apostles acted quickly to correct it (Acts 6), even appointing a "committee" to ensure that it wouldn't happen again.

Let us work together, and follow their example. If those who claim to be the people of God lead the way, then perhaps the rest of the world will follow. And who knows? Maybe they'll become Christians and be saved as well.

Cost #3: False Unity

Having observed the state of our divided religious world, how shall we respond? One proposed remedy for this situation has been the ecumenical movement, a series of cooperative efforts between denominations, dissimilar bodies that don't believe in the same things. They may go by such names as "interfaith councils" or "ministerial associations." Sometimes clergymen of different traditions will preach from each other's pulpits, or allow their members to take communion in the other's churches. Or a group of local congregations will band together for citywide revivals, and preach a compromise message that doesn't contradict any one church's beliefs more than absolutely necessary.

But at the end of the day, what has this really accomplished? After so much talk of a universal "brotherhood in Christ," the divisions between the groups remain. The following Sunday, the people scatter to their own separate places of worship. Each of the participating churches retains its own identity, creeds, and organization. And, of course, few of the people would ever dream of leaving their own church to join the other.

The largest ecumenical organization is the World Council of Churches, based in Geneva, Switzerland. Their membership consists of 347 denominations from nearly every Christian tradition, from 120 countries. Their creed, called *Faith and Order,* outlines a very specific plan of salvation. And yet, many of their member organizations believe very differently—but they retain the affiliation year after year.

The appeal of the ecumenical movement is understandable, because it gives the *appearance* of unity. Surely, the wall of hostility that formerly kept these people apart is coming down, and this is a good thing...isn't it? Of course it is. But at what cost? How much are you willing to compromise your convictions, simply to gain the approval of men?

Every time that a new faction is formed, the true worship of God is diminished. And our witness to the world is compromised. Ultimately, genuine unity will never be achieved through compromise or negotiation, as is the common method of choice today.

Cost #4: Unbelieving Masses

This gloomy outlook is not merely the personal judgment of some religious researcher, who poses leading questions to assure a predetermined outcome. This issue was on the mind of our Lord on the night of his betrayal:

May they [His followers] be brought to complete unity, to let the world know that you have sent me...[parenthetical comments mine] (John 17:23)

Jesus understood human nature. He knew what would attract followers to his movement; *unity* among the fellowship would be essential. Sadly, many of us fail to understand this; instead, we celebrate separation and the diversity of thought that it brings. But this type of "diversity" does not always draw us nearer to God.

As has often been said, the cost of a divided church is an unbelieving world. We could be out there fishing for men, but instead we end up quarreling amongst ourselves and choosing up sides. The unbelievers are watching, and they don't like what they see. When faced with so many choices, many of these seekers find that "truth" seems to be so elusive and subjective. They're confused, and they choose to choose none. Or they may visit a church because they know it's the right thing to do, but they still don't know what makes it different from the one down the street. But they should.

And if you're a member of a church, so should you.

Details, Details...Does it really matter?

Surely, in our modern religious world, anyone who rejects a liberal ecumenical approach is sure to be labeled as narrow-minded or divisive, even arrogant. We fancy ourselves a Christian nation, with our civil codes modeled after the dictates of divine law. *In God We Trust,* our currency proclaims, as our children—even in public schools—declare each morning with hand over heart that we are *One Nation Under God.* But somehow in recent years it has become a shameful thing to speak and act as if we actually believe it!

Having learned the truth, are we not duty-bound to obey it and hold each other accountable? If not, then there is no hope for any of us. In time, the Word of God will become entirely irrelevant, having been sacrificed at the altar of our respective sectarian traditions.

CHAPTER 14

the powerless church

To the angel of the church in Sardis write:...I know your deeds; you have a reputation of being alive, but you are dead. Wake up! Strengthen what remains and is about to die, for I have not found your deeds complete in the sight of my God. Remember, therefore, what you have received and heard; obey it, and repent. But if you do not wake up, I will come like a thief, and you will not know at what time I will come to you.
(Jesus, Revelation 3:1–3)

The present situation reveals the task that we have before us: All over our nation, churches are dying. Denominations are bickering among themselves and splintering; shrinking parishes are merged. In most organizations among men, it's no secret that 80% of the work is done by less than 20% of the people. The same could be said of many churches as well. Members are kept on the rolls for years after they've disappeared, which can conceal the problem, but only for so long. Without a doubt, many of our churches are bursting at the seams with eager seekers, more than at any other time in our history. Overall, however, it's plain to see that the level of religious *commitment* in America is not keeping pace.

Church-hopping and "truancy" have reached epidemic proportions. People move from one church to another at whim, as casually as they might change brands of laundry detergent. This should not be surprising, since most of us tend to think they're all pretty much the same, and are content to remain little more than pew-sitters.

According to a survey of Evangelical churches by the Barna Research Group,[16] 80% of their new members are either the children of existing members, or transfers from another congregation within the same fellowship. In other words, it is a rare event for them to admit a new member from "off the street," so to speak. In this way, the church becomes a closed society that exists almost entirely for the benefit of its existing members. It has no mission, no real concern for the lost. And their impact on the unchurched masses beyond their walls is practically nil.

Meaningless Membership

At the age of six months, I was baptized in a church that is steeped in many holy traditions. But for many years after leaving this congregation, my family continued to get mail from them regularly. Apparently, we were still on the books as members in good standing. So the pastor thanked us for our continued support of their ministry, and asked us to donate to the latest fundraiser.

At our new church, just down the street, they

published a new membership roster about every two years. It consistently listed around 200 names and addresses of members. Funny thing, though. This directory, in each successive edition, included dozens of people who—over the course of nine years—I never met. Even on the one occasion when they issued a directory with pictures, there were still quite a few that I couldn't identify. There were many people who rarely, if ever, showed up for meetings.

How to account for the phantom entries? In some cases, married *couples* (and all of their children) were listed and counted individually, even if only one of them was actually active in the fellowship. For others, they were veteran members who moved hundreds of miles away long ago and wanted to stay connected. Altogether, I can remember counting about forty people—or 20%—who attended the worship service on any given Sunday. This was puzzling to me, but I never dared to question it out loud at the time. What did I know? I was just a kid at the time.

For many years the Southern Baptist Convention has been recognized as the largest Protestant denomination in the U.S., reporting 15 million members. Sure, this is an impressive number, but what does it really mean? According to one recent study,[17] only about half this number was classified as active members. And what constitutes an "active" member? For the purposes of the survey, it was defined as a person (having already been admitted to membership) who had attended *one* meeting, or contributed *one* dollar, in the previous 12 months.

So we are left with about 7½ million "active" members. Of these, how many actually attend a worship service in the course of any given week? No one seems to know. Apparently, there has been no large-scale effort to make such an assessment.

Drive-Thru Religion

Has your church been blessed with a fruitful ministry? If so, then by all means praise God for His faithfulness. No doubt many churches are actually *losing* people year after year, so it looks like you're doing something right. But if we only get them in the door and pronounce them saved, the job is only half-done. The *second* half of the Great Commission (Matt. 28:20) commands us to "teach them (the newly converted) to obey everything I have commanded you."

Can this be done in a day? A week? A month? When we consider that so many of our existing members may be poorly trained in their beliefs, it doesn't seem right to hurry the process. This command clearly requires us to cultivate an ongoing relationship with these new recruits. We have a duty to nurture them to maturity. Be vulnerable, share from our own lives, and get our hands dirty if need be.

Unfortunately, in our own generation, "drive-thru" conversions have become all too common. Often, people get baptized—or answer an altar call—and then disappear shortly afterward, never to be seen again. We sincerely believe that our duty is done, and they don't understand why it's so important to stick around. Why don't they know? Often, it's because we didn't tell them. We wouldn't want to be too legalistic or demanding, you know.

Nothing new: This phenomenon was seen at the Cane Ridge Revival. The leaders did not provide any type of ongoing support system for their new converts. They did not organize into a church and did not provide Bible instruction. Once the meeting was over, it was over. Truly converted or not, the people were basically cast adrift to fend for themselves.

This also happens in churches that boast hundreds of baptisms each year. In many places, you can simply walk in the door and get baptized upon request, at the drop of a hat. This "outpatient" service may come with little or no instruction, and no expectation of a future commitment.

My Brother's Keeper? The Scriptures employ many useful metaphors to describe a Christian fellowship—a church is described as a "family," a fellow believer is called a "brother" (or "sister"), and a conversion is termed a "new birth."

In many places, however, this symbolism only goes so far. If your daughter or your sister didn't come home for dinner for weeks at a time, would you not be concerned and go out looking for her? Tragically, many of these runaways never return. Worse, the families often don't recognize that there's a problem.

Have you ever observed the mega-church in your community and been impressed by their success? They have 5- or 10- or 15,000 members, starting from a couple hundred just a few short years ago. How, pray tell, did they do it? Often, they may be counting a large number of people who experienced these hurry-up conversions. They are names on a list, who displayed an interest in heavenly matters at one time—not necessarily people in pews *today*.

Blame-shifting

When observing the decline of Western civilization and the weakening of religious devotion within American households, churches have given many reasons. One of the more commonly cited candidates is our popular culture, which influences our children to engage in all kinds of immoral behavior. And it certainly has. But this is hardly a recent development, because every generation of believers has had distractions of its own.

Our first-century brothers lived in a society that celebrated the atrocities of the Roman arena; we have religious sects that blow up cars and buildings. The Roman theater provided entertainment that was every bit as graphic and immoral as any movie that you've ever seen. They were tempted by the pleasures of alcoholism, gluttony, and prostitution. But today, we sophisticated moderns have learned from the lessons of the past. Instead, we are tempted by um, oh yeah, alcoholism, gluttony, and prostitution.

Sports. In some places, churches with low attendance have gone so far as to blame the professional sports leagues for scheduling games on Sunday. For if there were no baseball or football games on the Lord's Day (so the argument goes) then certainly more people would find themselves in pews instead of grandstands or armchairs. Couldn't the leagues display some social conscience, and play on Tuesday instead?

Ah, if only it were so easy to produce faithful Christians.

Yes, we live in a world of many choices. There are plenty of things that we can do on the weekend. Sporting events, movies, concerts, and amusement parks all vie for our attention. We can go fishing or camping, or simply sleep until noon. And all of these things lure people away from their commitments to God. But many of us don't recognize this trend, because we count as fruits of our ministry:

- Members who haven't shown up for a worship service for years;
- Many who are leading immoral lifestyles, but we don't know because we're not paying attention;
- People instantly "converted" at revival meetings, and never return; and
- Legions of infants and small children who will never be confirmed.

Do we really have the right to exhort the flock to be more like Jesus, while we lie to ourselves and the outside world with these misleading and artificially-inflated numbers? Do we actually want our people to come to church on Sunday simply out of habit, or *just because they have nothing else to do?* No! The

Christian life is about self-control. And discipline. And setting priorities in your schedule.

God and Mammon

At one time, it was taken for granted that the average American church member contributed about 10% of his income to his church. This was called a *tithe,* derived from an Old English word for "one-tenth." Recent research, however, indicates that the "sacrifice" has declined to about 2.5%. This is a smaller portion, per-capita, than during the Great Depression.[18]

Certainly, this is not because we can't afford to give more. At the dawn of the 21st century we're most spoiled nation on Earth; we always seem to have sufficient cash flow to buy PDA's, designer suits, $5.00 cups of gourmet coffee, and sport sedans with anti-lock brakes. How can this be, at a time when our nation is both more religious *and* more prosperous than ever before?

Maybe it's because we have such low expectations of our new converts. We tell them "come forward, pray Jesus into your heart, and you're saved." Just like that, presto-change-o, suddenly you're a new man. Come to church when you feel like it, drop a buck or two in the collection plate if you can. We tell them all about the blessings and promises that flow from their salvation, and how wonderful it's going to be when we meet Jesus in Heaven.

But we're reluctant to make any further demands, for fear of chasing them away. So we tell them very little, if anything, about the sacrifices and responsibilities it brings. We lead them to God with instant conversions and low expectations. In the end, you get what you pay for. Churches are rapidly becoming irrelevant in their members' lives, and these issues (attendance and money) are but the most obvious manifestations of the trend.

Ineffective Evangelism

Searching for guidance over the course of many years, I visited dozens of churches, sometimes driving over fifty miles from home. I came forward for the altar call time after time, searching for guidance and redemption, and met a great number of very nice people. As far as I could tell, they were quite devout and sincere. They congratulated me on my desire to follow God, and directed me to a handful of encouraging passages from the Bible, such as John 3:16 or Jeremiah 29:11–14.

And *then...?*

They walked away.

No one seemed to care what became of me after that first meeting, even when I gave them my address and phone number. If I tried to demonstrate my eagerness by attending the Sunday worship service week after week, it didn't seem to make a difference. *No one* ever called me, came to visit me, or asked me out to lunch after the church service. If I missed a week, *no one* seemed to notice. *No one* ever attempted to teach me the Bible. At a time when I needed them the most, they were gone. Apparently, their work was done, and I was left to wonder what was going on.

Did I do something wrong? Was I expecting too much?

Once again, just as in the "family" illustration at chapter 7, I became homeless. Each time I got myself "reborn," I ended up an orphan. No one wanted to take me home or accept responsibility for my instruction or well-being. Sure, I was always welcome to return; but as a spiritual latch-key kid, I had to fend for myself.

Often, ironically, these were revival meetings that had been advertised far and wide for weeks in advance. This was citywide evangelism at its best, as they cast a wide net to bring in as many as possible. Dozens of people had worked so hard to prepare for this day. And yet, somehow, they often (apparently) believed that their responsibility ended at the altar.

How Ya Gonna Keep 'em Down on the Farm, Once They've Seen Paris?

It was a pivotal moment in the history of Israel. The elders approached Samuel with a demand: *we want you to appoint a king to lead us*. This distressed the prophet greatly. "You don't know what you're asking," he explained. "A king will draft your sons for his army, your daughters as household servants, and demand a share of your crops. That's just what kings *do*" (paraphrase mine).

Even so, the elders persisted in their plea:

> "No!" they said. "We want a king over us. Then we will be like all the other nations, with a king to lead us and to go out before us and fight our battles."
>
> (1 Samuel 8:19–20)

The Israelites were looking over the fence, where the grass always seemed greener. The pagans were so much happier, or so it appeared. I can only imagine what their continual groaning might sound like in the ears of the Almighty:

*Sure, we know that we're God's chosen people. Yeah, Grampa told us all about how the Lord rescued us from the hand of Pharaoh and all that, ten laws, ten plagues, ten curtains in the tabernacle, yada, yada, yada. Whatever. We've heard the speech a thousand times before. Get a move on already, we've got dinner reservations in Gomorrah. We want to be like **them**, we've got to see how the other half lives.*

So Samuel inquired of the Lord and eventually gave in, appointing Saul as the first king of Israel.

You may have heard this story in Sunday School. Like me, you probably scorned the elders for their short-sighted foolishness. You snickered under your breath, thinking *I told you so* when Saul (and the majority of his successors) turned out to be worldly and corrupt. *When will these people ever learn?* But in modern times, despite this warning, this is exactly what has happened in Christian churches around the world.

Don't believe it? Just look around.

In every generation since the beginning, we have made great compromises to make the faith more attractive. Standards of morality and lifestyle have been watered down to a level that our Messiah would never recognize. But just as in the days of

Samuel, the people of God are called upon to be *different,* a leavening influence within our society.

The divorce rate among believers (around 50%) is now about the same as that of our population as a whole. Abortion, the killing of innocent children, is no longer a moral issue; instead it has become a "choice," a sacred civil right and a matter of personal preference. Anyone who holds strong convictions about these things is bound to be labeled as "bigoted" or "intolerant"—by fellow Christians! Political correctness prevails, even among those who profess to be the followers of the most politically incorrect person in history.

The tail wags the dog. Jesus established His church because He wanted to change the world. Instead, what has happened in many quarters is that the world has changed the church. He taught a Gospel of black-and-white, while many of us (both then and now) would rather believe in a thousand shades of gray. Nope, you don't get to blame these outside influences for the decline of our religious institutions.

The Christians are looking over the fence, and they long to be where the grass seems greener. We have met the enemy, and it is us.

Warfare, Spiritual and Otherwise

During the Spanish Civil War (1936–39), the battle lines were drawn between the government's Popular Front party and the rebel Nationalists. The resistance was led by General Emilio Mola Vidal, and his army was composed of four units, or *columns.*

General Francisco Franco, initially reluctant to get involved, went on to lead the revolt in the South.

In a radio address to the populace, Mola declared that an upcoming offensive on the city of Madrid would be led by a *quinta columna,* or "fifth column."

The *fifth?* Has he forgotten that *cinco* is more than *cuatro?*

Actually, the general was showing himself to be a shrewd student of warfare. The capital city was already infiltrated with rebel sympathizers (a "fifth column") who supported his cause, and they would convert yet more traitors. *Propaganda,* appealing to the dreams and ambitions of the people, proved every bit as effective as bullets and brawn. The city eventually fell, and the insiders were given much of the credit for the victory.

Every Christian should take heed, because we still need to deal with a few Fifth Columns of our own.

- One such column tells us that Jesus isn't the only way.
- The next tells us, "All you have to do is believe."
- Another whispers into our ear, ever so softly, "The Bible isn't really true."
- Still others beckon with the promise of riches, fame, sex, and worldly success.

In a momentous encounter with Peter, Jesus proclaimed that the gates of Hades would never prevail against His church. No outside force would ever be able to destroy it. These inspiring words should be a source of great confidence for us all. But we're not out of the woods yet, because the greatest threat to the Kingdom of God does not come from foreign invaders. Instead, like the assault on Madrid, the danger is from within. Or in the words of one of our greatest presidents:

> *America will never be destroyed from the outside. If we falter and lose our freedoms, it will be because we destroyed ourselves.*
>
> (Abraham Lincoln)

The gates of our churches have been breached, my friend. Unbelievers and skeptics abound, and in modern times they have gained much influence and respectability as they go about recruiting allies to take up their cause. They gain entry not by Trojan horse or battering ram, but by simply walking in the front door. We promote them to positions of authority, enjoying their sermons of easy believism and painless discipleship. Their weapons are not sword and spear, but logic, emotion, and half-truths. Yet when they preach a false gospel, their hands are stained with the blood of the saints just the same. And when Christians don't take their lives and doctrine seriously, they become easy prey. Maybe this has already happened in your community.

A Personal Note

Upon reading this book, some may be inclined to believe that I have been unduly critical in my assessments of various people and movements. After all, couldn't I just make my point without naming names? Sure I could.

But that would be dishonest, and a great disservice to you. Again, I am constrained by my earliest lessons about writing: I have a duty to cite my sources and back up my assertions, so that you can verify it for yourself. For it does little good to simply expound generalized theories in a vacuum; specific case studies are needed. These anecdotes are not just about the unique isolated problems of a little neighborhood church somewhere in Podunkville, USA. Rather, they exist within perfectly respectable mainline denominations that have influenced millions of people around the world. This is central to my thesis, and without it there's no point in writing a book.

Therefore, the telling of this story is not entirely an academic exercise. It's also very much a personal matter, and somewhat therapeutic at that. As you might imagine from reading this book, I have often been called upon to answer for my "unconventional" beliefs. And I stubbornly held my ground.

But far too often, both for my dogmatism and pride, I was wrong.

At my own church, a non-denominational congregation in Southern California, these past few years have been a time of much introspection and change. After doing business the same way for decades (and with great success), it became apparent that our "business as usual" was no longer working. Gradually, some of the old assumptions were being openly questioned and reconsidered for the first time. Not that they were entirely wrong, but they were just that—*assumptions* that we hadn't fully examined. And for many years I blindly defended the institution, truly believing that we had it all together.

But I was wrong.

Which is not to say that we were about to renounce our fundamental teachings. We were quite confident of our doctrine, and the mission remained clear. But how to get there? How exactly to implement the Great Commission? *That* was the $64,000 question.

No doubt, I have felt the sting of persecution. Surely, it is quite tempting to dismiss criticism as the wild rants of evil people who have nothing better to do. But guess what? Sometimes it's not really "persecution" at all, and the people aren't really evil. Sometimes they're right, and we desperately need to change.

As it turned out, we had to slay a few Giant Pink Elephants of our own. Things like hero worship, legalism, and a bureaucratic corporate structure that prevented local leaders from truly serving the needs of their people. Some of our iconoclastic "tradition-busting" ways actually made us slaves to a slew of newly crystallized traditions—the very thing that we had sought to escape. With this new understanding the future looks bright, and we can once again get on with the business of making disciples for Christ.

EPILOGUE
the road ahead

They devoted themselves to the apostles' teaching and to the fellowship, to the breaking of bread and to prayer. Everyone was filled with awe, and many wonders and miraculous signs were done by the apostles. All the believers were together and had everything in common. Selling their possessions and goods, they gave to anyone as he had need. Every day they continued to meet together in the temple courts. They broke bread in their homes and ate together with glad and sincere hearts, praising God and enjoying the favor of all the people. And the Lord added to their number daily those who were being saved.
(Acts 2:42–47)

On one historic occasion, when Jesus granted to Peter the keys to the Kingdom, eleven witnesses were present. Later, at Pentecost, when the time came for the Prince of the Apostles to use the keys, *thousands* would bear witness to the establishment of this new kingdom. It was not the earthly empire that some were expecting, which would bring them political power and social prestige. Not a place on a map, but a place in the hearts of men. The Roman occupation would not be ending any time soon, as they had hoped. The mighty conqueror, clad in heavy iron mail and rushing into battle on his regal white steed, never appeared; but that was beside the point because it wasn't supposed to be *that* kind of kingdom. The ministry of Jesus was so unconventional, in fact, that he defied all expectations and confounded all the experts. To this day he remains the proverbial "prophet without honor" in his own homeland.

Still, God's purposes on this day would be fulfilled. "Repent and be baptized," Peter urged them, for this was the way of the new kingdom. "Save yourselves from this corrupt generation," he pleaded, and they could become citizens of the realm. This was to be the way of salvation, the new birth, adoption into the family of God.

Passover, the annual occasion for more and more bloody sacrifices, became a communal meal (the Lord's Supper) with *symbolic* blood, in observance of a once-for-all-time sacrifice already made.

Previously, the blood of a lamb (on a wooden doorpost) had saved the Sons of Abraham from physical death at the hand of the destroying angel. From henceforth, the blood of *the* Lamb (on a wooden cross) would save them from eternal damnation at the hand of a jealous God. Pentecost would no longer be observed for its harvest of wheat and rye at the swing of a sickle, but instead for the harvest of three thousand human souls at the turn of a key. This became the fulfillment of all that the prophets had foretold. Even Moses, himself denied entry into the Promised Land, longed to see such a glorious day.

How Did They Do It?

There is much that we can learn from the earliest Christians, during and immediately after the age of the apostles. We seem to forget what it was that Jesus originally expected of his followers. A few examples, in no particular order:

Fellowship. Conversion, salvation, and baptism were typically simultaneous events; church membership and regular attendance naturally followed.

Lifestyle. Every Christian was expected to follow a lifestyle that was characterized by self-denial, obedience, and sacrifice.

Unity. The members had disagreements over doctrinal issues, just like you and I still face today. But if you and your closest friends were in the midst of facing the lions in the Roman arena, would you be concerned about winning the argument? Nah, me either. Accordingly, these early congregations enjoyed an intimate level of fellowship that many of us will never experience.

Persecution. It was a dangerous thing to follow Jesus. These stalwarts had to meet with the utmost of secrecy, sometimes in underground burial chambers called catacombs. Those who refused to deny the faith could be subjected to harassment, discrimination, confiscation of their property, even death. It was just a part of the package, and they all understood it. No wimps need apply.

Sound doctrine. They encountered plenty of false teachers, just like you and I do today. But for all of their lies and half-truths, the heretics actually *benefited* the churches in a way that no one could have expected. When confronted with several "alternative" theologies, the believers were forced to *think* and to *choose*. So the flock was thinned, and the remaining group was stronger and more committed than before.

Happily, we still have a chance to return to this original purity.

The Challenge

> *Now therefore fear the Lord, and serve him in sincerity and in truth...choose you this day whom ye will serve; whether the gods which your fathers served that were on the other side of the flood* [river], *or the gods of the Amorites, in whose land ye dwell: but as for me and my house, we will serve the Lord.*
>
> (Joshua 24:14–15, KJV)

If you knew that you would die today, what would be your final words to your family? What would be on your mind, that you felt compelled to share it in your dying breath? Maybe you would remind your son to take his place as the man of the house. Or to bring in the crops in the spring. Perhaps you would leave instructions about the disposition of your worldly goods. As for me, I can only imagine that a million things would come to mind, each one jockeying for position on my tongue.

For the great men of the Bible, this was no difficult decision. Moses called upon the Lord to bless the tribes of Israel, that they might be faithful and prosperous. Elijah (although technically, he didn't exactly *die*) passed down a double portion of his spirit, to his protégé. For Jesus, he issued a call to world evangelism.

And then we come to the last words of Joshua, in his final address to the Children of Israel. The sojourn of Joshua is a cautionary tale for believers in all ages, for it shows us that even the chosen people can go so terribly astray, without ever knowing it. Among an apostate generation, he took a stand against the accepted religious norms of the day and drew a line in the sand that posed a challenge to every believer. His message? You're the people of God, *not* of this world, and don't you ever forget it again. Stay faithful, no matter what anyone else around you might do.

Mind you, these are the people who crossed the Red Sea on foot. They ate manna and quail from heaven, drank water from the rock, and personally witnessed so many miracles of God. They were forgiven of their idolatry and ingratitude time after time. And they had entered the Promised Land! You might think that such a people would have a natural love for God, and this sermon wouldn't be necessary.

But still, they lost their way.

So at this critical juncture, Joshua called upon his people to make *choices:* Are you in, or are you out? No halfway measures would do. You're free to do whatever you like, of course, but at least be honest about it and *make up your mind.* Sitting on the fence, accepting other religions as equally valid? Not an option.

Is this what you understood when you became a Christian—or did you simply "receive Jesus," or "join a church?" Were you taught a hard-line, uncompromising body of doctrine—or just a pleasant message of sunshine and rainbows? Again, if you're like me, it may be that you've never thought about it.

From a logical human standpoint, of course, Joshua's gambit was an incredibly risky proposition. Frankly, many clergymen these days are reluctant ask for such radical commitment. But Joshua wasn't concerned with filling the pews at the following Sabbath worship service. Instead, his mission was to defend the honor of God *today,* whether by many or by few. He could not know how many people would still be at his side tomorrow.

Have you ever heard a preacher speak so plainly?

Through it all, the history of the people of God has *always* been an endless cycle of rebellion and restoration—in every nation, in every age, and in every language and culture. Is it really so unreasonable to consider that we might be as unstable as they?

Fortunately, the Lord bestows His grace upon those of us who act in ignorance (1 Tim. 1:13–16). But grace is a double-edged sword: where enlightenment comes, responsibility follows. Once we've learned the truth, we will be held accountable (Acts 17:30). Would you expect anything less from a righteous God? Any other response can only be characterized as dishonest, a willful blindness from the facts.

For many of us, Jesus has become a paper tiger.

He's an omnipotent ruler who lays down the law with great authority—yet doesn't really require us to obey it. We subtly attribute him with human weaknesses, expecting Him not to *forgive* our sins, but instead to *excuse* them. In our Sunday School lessons, we observed that He punished the ungodly in spectacular ways—even raising up armies against *His own people* when they disobeyed.

Yet we can't imagine that we (since we count himself as his people) *could* be next.

Why Are We Here?

Why do we call ourselves Christians? Why do we have a church? As it happens, Jesus has already given us the only mission that we need: Reach out to a lost world, and show them the way. Preach, correct, rebuke, and encourage. Let God be true, and every man a liar. Make disciples, call 'em as you see 'em, and let the chips fall where they will.

We speak boldly enough about saving the world for Jesus, as we should. But if we are ever to fulfill this mission, we must call every one of our people to a meaningful level of doctrinal purity and personal righteousness. In many churches, only about half of the members attend a worship service in the course of a given week. Given this state of affairs, how can we ever hope to reach the world (or even pretend to believe in the goal) if we can't even get *our own people* to show up on Sunday morning?

There are many things that we might do in the course of our community outreach. Summer camps, soup kitchens, homeless shelters, twelve-step support groups, food pantries, bingo games, and so on. At the church of my youth, they hosted adult reading classes and took up an annual offering for the poor of the Third World. Surely, there's nothing wrong with these kinds of programs; they are, and should be, an important *part* of our mission. But why are we here to begin with? Are we truly fulfilling *the* mission? All of the socially-minded ministries in the world will never compensate for failed evangelism. How tragic it will be on the last day, if we save the bodies of our neighbors, yet lose their souls. Might as well dissolve the organization, turn over the keys to the United Way, and go home.

Jesus understood this weakness of human nature. When He called His disciples to a radical new level of devotion (John 6:25–70), many turned and fled. And he didn't beg them to return. We, who claim to be his followers, must likewise be prepared to recognize and confront this apostasy. Otherwise, we have no reason to be in business at all. No right to wear his name. Easy-believism, as popular as it is, can only pollute the fellowship of the saints. And it will never change the moral character of our society.

Are you up to this task? If so, then be prepared for resistance among the ranks. Through the ages, for every prophet who cries "repent," there have always been hordes of followers that howl in protest. They will assert their "freedom in Christ" and plead for a return to the comfortable status quo. Jesus died a grueling death on the cross in payment for our sins, and still the "enlightened" in our midst will warn of the dangers of doing too much for him in return. Wouldn't want to be accused of trying to earn our salvation, you know.

If our members should fail in these areas, then maybe it's because *we* have failed *them*.

The Thinking Man's Religion

> [A Pharisee asked,] "Teacher, which is the greatest commandment in the Law?" Jesus replied: "'Love the Lord your God with all your heart and with all your soul and with all your mind.' This is the first and greatest commandment."
>
> (Matthew 22:36–38)

Jesus taught his followers to practice a multifaceted religion. It was not exceedingly complicated, but at the same time not quite as simplistic as some would like to believe. He told us that we must worship God not only with heart and soul, but also with our *mind*. Not just with devotion and emotion, but also with our *intellect*. No doubt, we are told that faith means believing and trusting in things unseen (Heb. 11). Miracles, by their very nature, may never pass any test of scientific inquiry or mathematical calculation. He expects us to approach Him with reverence and awe, in a manner that none of us will ever fully understand this side of heaven.

Still, at the end of the day, your religious belief and practice must make sense to your *mind*. There should be evidences that appeal to your awareness of logic and good sense. You should be able to recognize superstition, wishful thinking, and circular reasoning when you see them. When you go to church, don't check your brain at the door.

This, I believe, is the forgotten virtue of Christianity.

No attorney would stay in business for long if he studied (or applied) only *a part* of the Penal Code. And yet many educated, intelligent Christians dare to approach the throne of God after studying only *a part* of the Gospel. No responsible person makes a significant life-changing decision on a whim. Even so, our college-trained church leaders continue to solicit instant conversions by the millions.

Paul often wrote of his longing to see his own people, the Jews, come to know Christ:

For I can testify about them that they are zealous for God, but their zeal is not based on knowledge. Since they did not know the righteousness that comes from God and sought to establish their own, they did not submit to God's righteousness.

(Romans 10:2–3)

The Israelites believed in God, and genuinely desired to serve Him. Unfortunately, like many of us, theirs was an *uninformed* enthusiasm. They wanted to do it their own way, and devotion gave way to compromise and disobedience. More than the population at large, we are especially vulnerable to the subtle lures of tradition, idolatry, and false confidence. Religion can be deceptive that way.

Of course, it really *could have been* much easier. The Gospel *could have been* handed down to us in a manner that wouldn't require us to work so hard. Some authoritative type like a Peter, or a Paul, could have produced a comprehensive "textbook" for us, to spell out these things in A-B-C order. Something like a missal or catechism, perhaps. It could give us a fixed liturgy for worship, and tell us exactly how to deal with every possible problem or situation we will ever face. Then, we wouldn't need to cross-reference so many Scriptures. We wouldn't have to think for ourselves. Everything would be spelled out in advance, and all we'd have to do is follow the "script."

But they *didn't* give us that kind of book. And frankly, I'm not so sure that we would necessarily be any better off if they had.

This is because basic human nature would remain. No matter how plain the message, men would attempt to "interpret" it to their own liking, just as they have done with the Bible. Centuries of tradition would still be observed without question. Governments would interfere, and schismatic groups would be formed. In other words, we'd have the same situation that already prevails today. Surely, the unquestioned obedience to "scripts" (creeds) has already caused us enough trouble.

Nay, I am convinced that our God actually wants us to reason and think for ourselves.

Physician, Heal Thyself!

As Christians, we strive to walk righteously before our God and avoid sin. But even the righteous man falls short from time to time. As we know, some sins are more obvious than others— theft, murder, falsehood, adultery. Most religions recognize these acts as sinful, and even the atheist—unbelieving though he may be—nonetheless possesses a certain intuitive sense of morality. (Even the evil Cain, while having no written law, nonetheless felt guilty after killing his brother.)

But the more devout you are—and the more that you attend church, pray, evangelize, tithe, or read your Bible—the harder it will be to recognize that something in your spiritual discipline *could,* in itself, be contrary to the will of God. Wasn't this the lesson that we learned from Aaron's sons, when they burned incense improperly and were consumed by the fire (Lev. 10)? Or from the example of Ananias and Sapphira, who were struck dead when they deceitfully offered money to the apostles (Acts 5)?

This widespread confusion is understandable. We modern believers are much more "sophisticated" than ever before. We have access to so many sources of information, so many points of view. We're more careful, we ask more questions, we require more evidence. In just the last few generations, we have become more and more distrustful of anyone who attempts to preach in *absolutes.* And that might actually be a *good* thing, except that it also means we carry more baggage.

There is a malady that confronts every person who desires to follow in the path of Jesus, and it is essential that we understand it. For as we have seen, once we begin this discussion, it inescapably leads into a myriad of other issues. We are forced to reconsider so many other assumptions about our religion. Things like teaching authority. Spiritual gifts. Commitment. The hazards of tradition. The deceitfulness of our emotions. Free will and personal responsibility. And the meaning of a genuine Christian conversion.

Upon examining the record of history, it becomes clear that we have placed our trust in many of the wrong things. So many of our cherished beliefs and practices were not established until centuries after the lifetimes of the apostles!

Still, the salvation of the world is within our grasp—but only if we undertake a fresh assessment to determine just how well we've done so far. Is there a large disparity between your membership total and your weekly attendance? If so, then maybe you've been a little too "open-minded" in your understanding of what it means to be a Christian. While each of us can (and should) have a small part in this process of self-examination, it will not be easy.

But first, we must admit that we have a problem.

Conclusion

So there you have it, my story in 52,000 words or less. Perhaps you had a different experience, and came to know the truth at a much younger age, with less hubbub along the way. You made an informed decision from the start, from which you have never retreated. To that I say: *hallelujah!* The world needs more people like you. Still, I've met enough people to know that I am certainly not unique.

Who am I? I am neither a Bible scholar nor a theologian, and do not have any special revelation from God. I have never fancied myself as anything more than a Christian who wants to know the truth. So again, please don't take my word for it. Everything on these pages is public information, and so easy to verify.

Please don't misunderstand me: I am *not* suggesting that everyone should believe as I do. And I'm certainly not trying to gather followers for a new movement. Indeed, I'm every bit as mortal as the next guy, and may in fact be harboring a few wild notions of my own. I ask only that you join the discussion, have an opinion, ask lots of questions, and don't settle for the simplistic pat answers. *Make up your m*ind as to what you believe in, know why you believe it, and don't be afraid of controversy. This is important, not just for your own sake, but because—sooner or later—you'll probably be in a position to teach someone else (1 Tim 4:16). Disagreement is one thing; *inertia,* fear of introspection and the truth, is another.

This book originated as a study of baptism. But as you may recall from the Introduction, it wasn't intended to be a book at all. This ancient ordinance simply became a jumping-off point from which these other issues naturally flowed. This is perfectly appropriate, I suppose, since the preaching of this message has often led people to politely suggest that I do exactly that—take a flying leap.

And what a remarkable leap of faith it has been.

That fateful day at the library has changed me forever, for it caused me to undergo an epiphany that might never have happened any other way. If this material seems new to you (as it was for me), maybe it's because you have never really examined your religion. Frankly, many people never do. Perhaps, if you think it about it, you'll find that your Sunday School education (like mine) was quite incomplete. So do your own research, and do your own thinking.

Joshua's challenge still echoes for us today. We all have some tough choices to make. This is a bold and exciting adventure, and so full of promise. Are you ready?

Again, why do you believe what you believe? The answer to that question is vitally important, if we truly desire to serve God.

bibliography

Restoration Quarterly, "The Invitation: A Historical Survey," by Thomas Olbricht

Encyclopedia of Early Christianity, Everett Ferguson, Ed., 1998 Garland Publishing, Inc., New York, NY

When God Builds a Church, Bob Russell, 2000, Howard Publishing,

Commentary on the Book of Acts, F. F. Bruce, 1960 Eerdmans Publishing Co., Grand Rapids, MI

The Theology of Huldreich Zwingli, W. P. Stephens, 1986, Clarendon Press, Oxford

Churches and Church Membership in the U.S., 1990; Martin B. Bradley, et al; © 1992 by Glenmary Research Center, Atlanta, GA

Merriam-Webster's Collegiate Dictionary, Tenth Edition © 2002 by Merriam-Webster, Inc.

endnotes

1. "Laughing Out Loud," "Be Right Back," "By The Way," and "In My Humble Opinion," respectively.
2. For Aquinas, *Summa Theologica*. For Edwards, *The Great Christian Doctrine of Original Sin Defended*. For Henry, *Commentary at Acts 2:38*. For Knox, the *Scottish Confession*. For Luther, his *Small Catechism*. For Nee, *The Normal Christian Life*. For Wesley, *A Treatise on Baptism*.
3. Immaculate Conception, as proclaimed by the First Vatican Council, teaches that Mary was uniquely born without the stain of Original Sin; the virgin birth refers to the miraculous birth of Jesus.
4. He's not. It was not until many years after his death, and against his own wishes, that a church institution was established in his name.
5. *Introduction to Romans,* from Luther's German translation of the Bible.
6. http://www.nonprofitpages.com/elm/jm_fgg.htm, retrieved 1/5/06
7. Published by Creation House, 1987
8. *Exodus: Why Americans Are Fleeing Liberal*

Churches for Conservative Christianity, Sentinel Publishers, 2005

[9] A cheapjack is a dealer in junk merchandise.

[10] But this poses yet another problem, because the release from purgatory depends on the prayers of people on earth. This theory became one of the theological underpinnings of Indulgences in the first place.

[11] Augustine, *On the Merits and Remission of Sins, and on the Baptism of Infants*

[12] "The more things change, the more they stay the same," Attributed to Alphonse Karr, French poet and journalist, 1808–1890.

[13] The origin of this quotation, whether in a sermon or published essay, is unclear. Still, it is well attested in historical documents.

[14] Oxford University Press, 2000

[15] *Churches and Church Membership in the U.S., 1990*; Martin B. Bradley, et al

[16] *Grow Your Church From The Outside In,* by George Barna, 2002.

[17] Founders Journal, (Issue 19/20, Winter/Spring 1995) *Southern Baptists at the Crossroads, by Thomas Ascol.*

[18] That is, as a percentage of disposable (after-tax) income. Survey conducted by empty tomb, inc.

Contact Steven Hutson at
steve@hutson.net
or order more copies of this book at:

TATE PUBLISHING, LLC

127 East Trade Center Terrace
Mustang, Oklahoma 73064

(888) 361 - 9473

TATE PUBLISHING, LLC
www.tatepublishing.com